Landscapes Coloring Book for Adults

An Advanced Adult Coloring Book of 40 Realistic Landscapes by various artists

Adult Coloring World

ISBN-13: 978-1519622839

ISBN-10: 151962283X

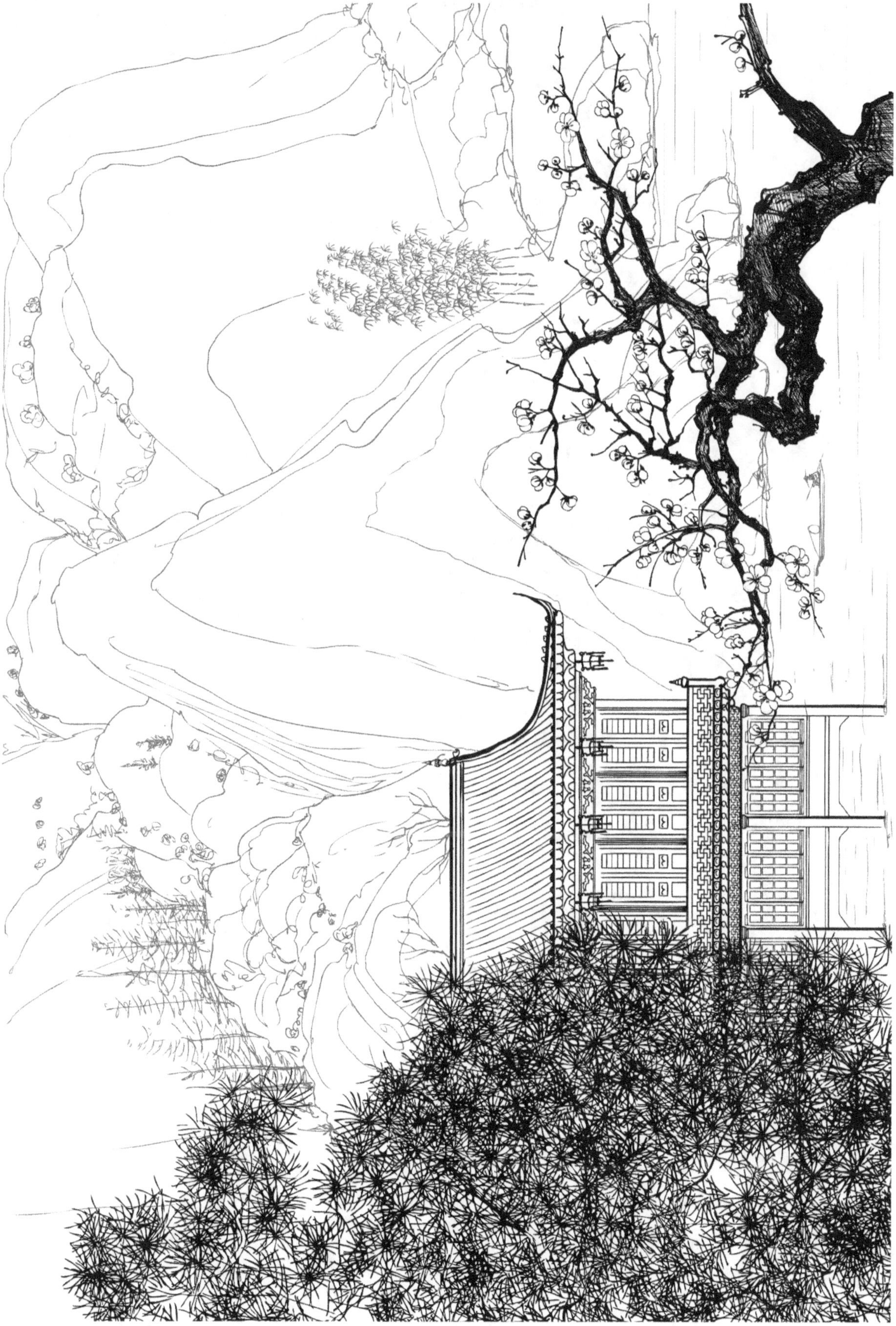

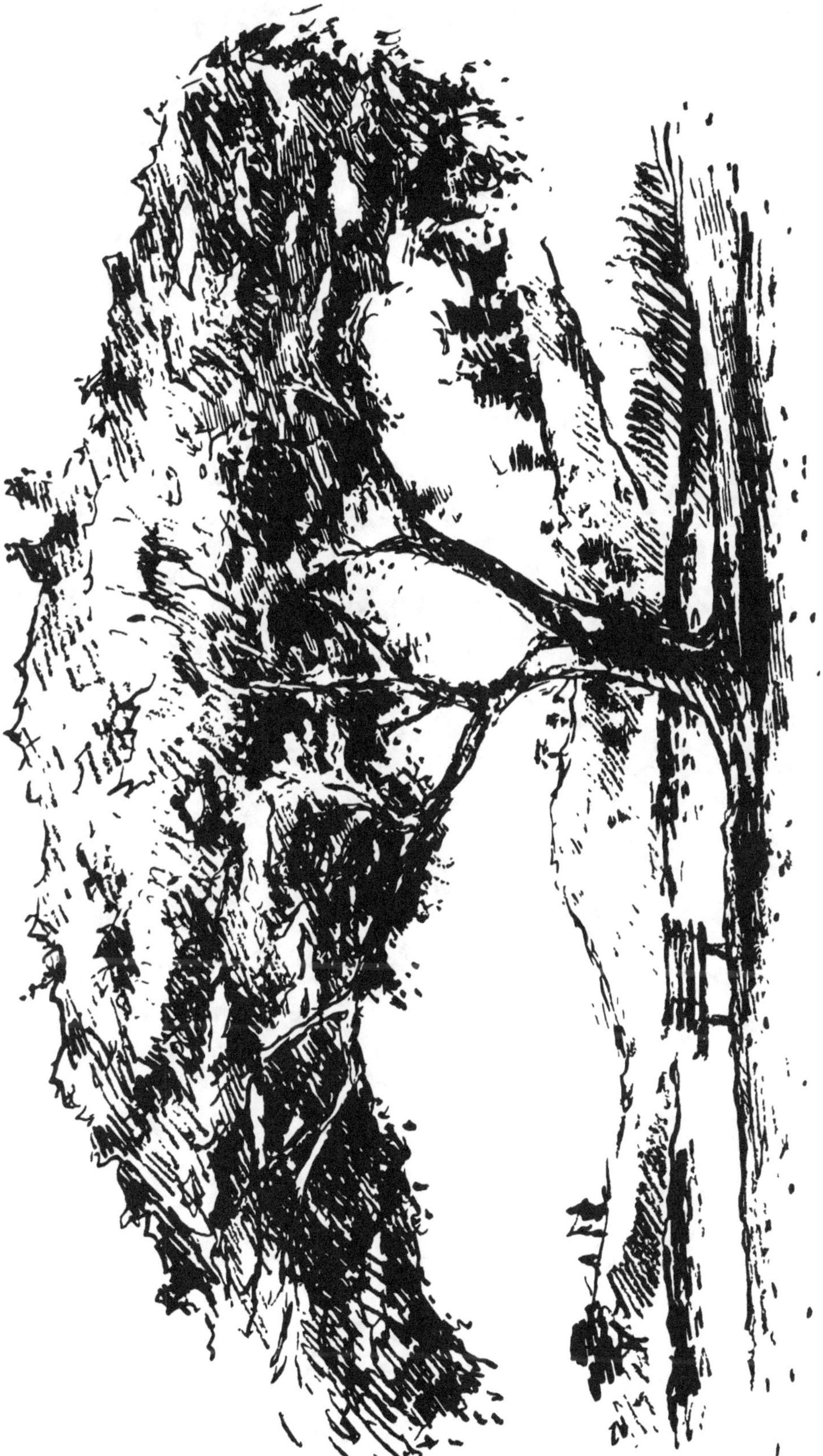

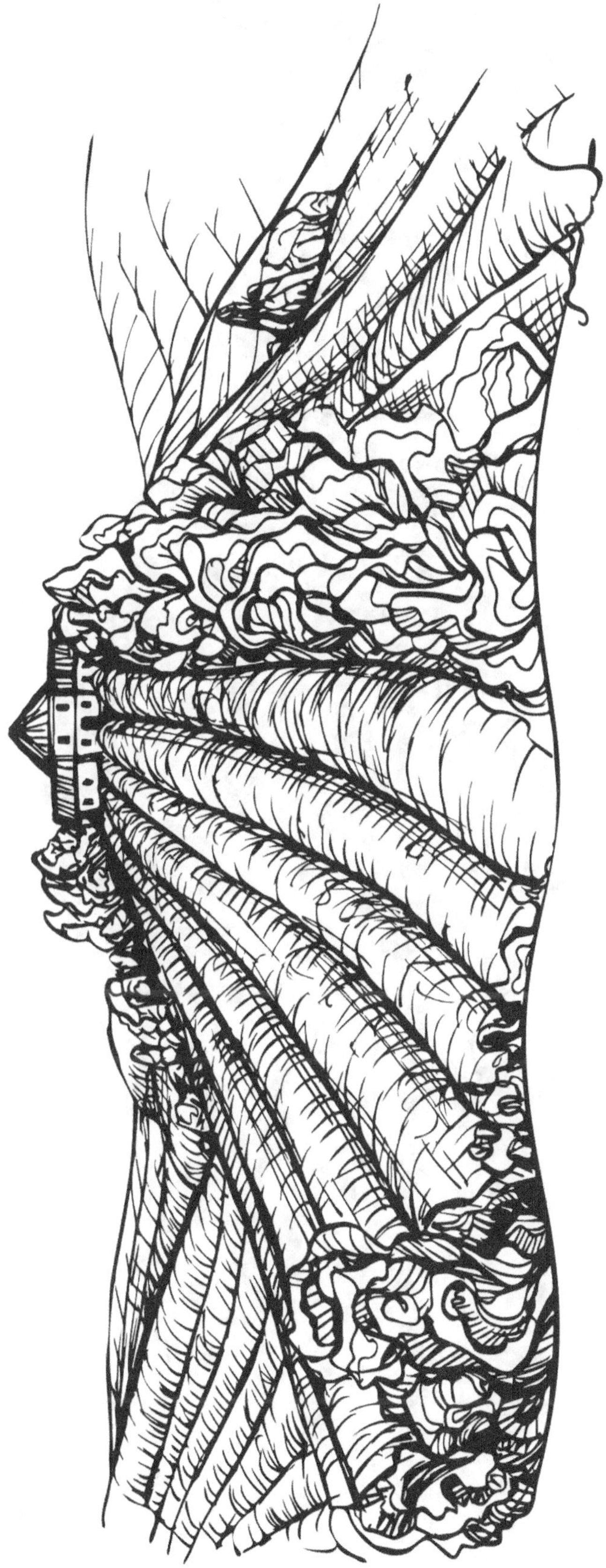

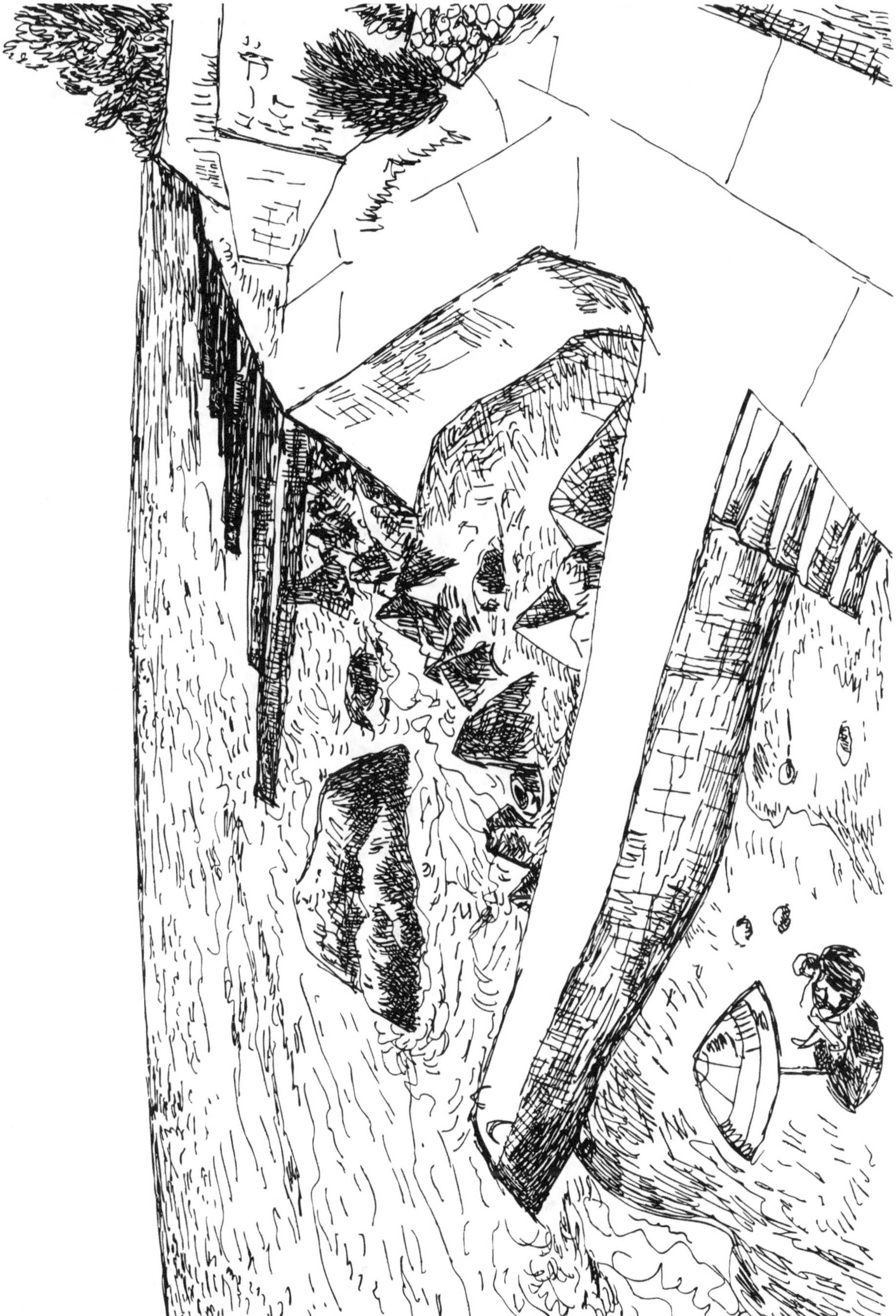

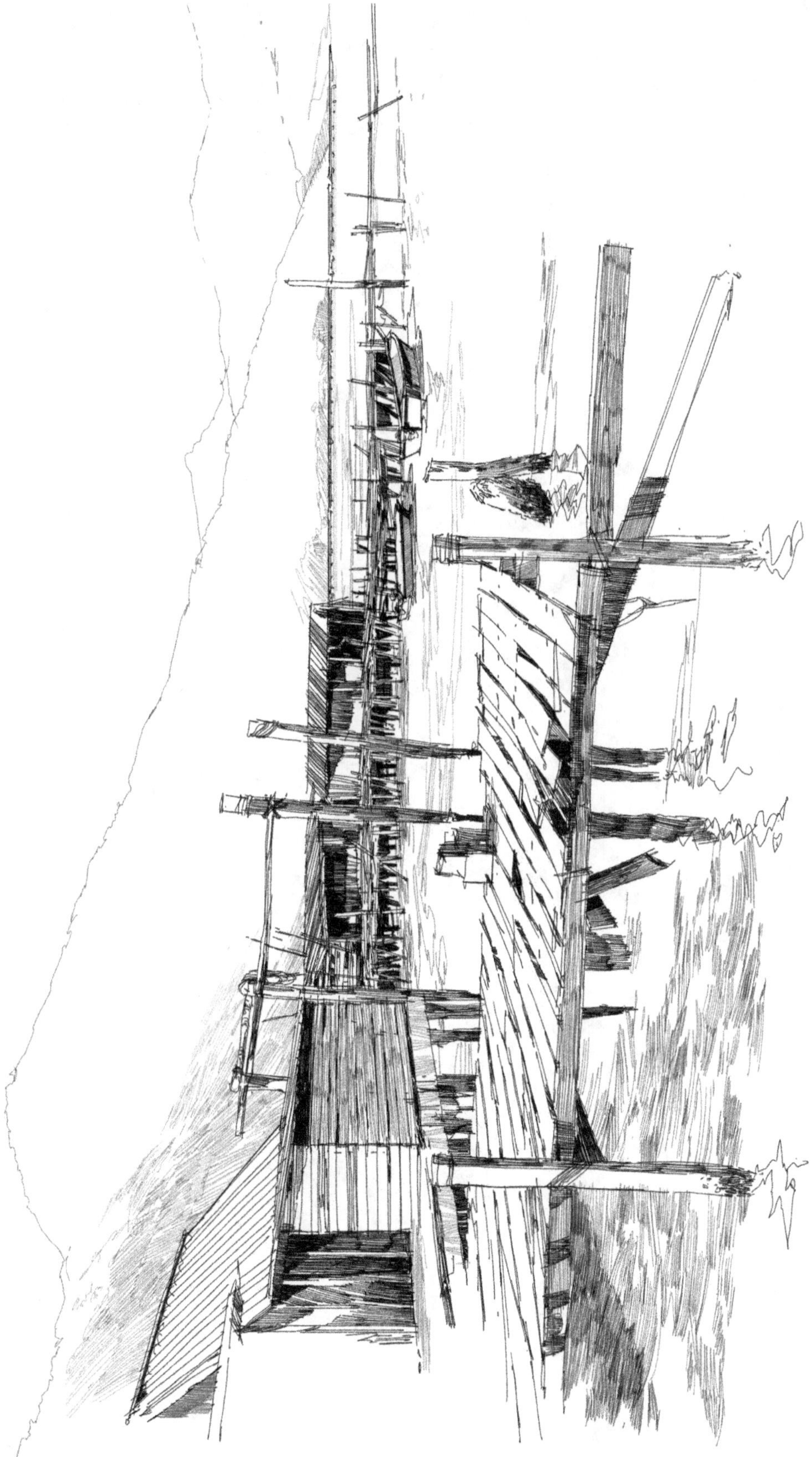

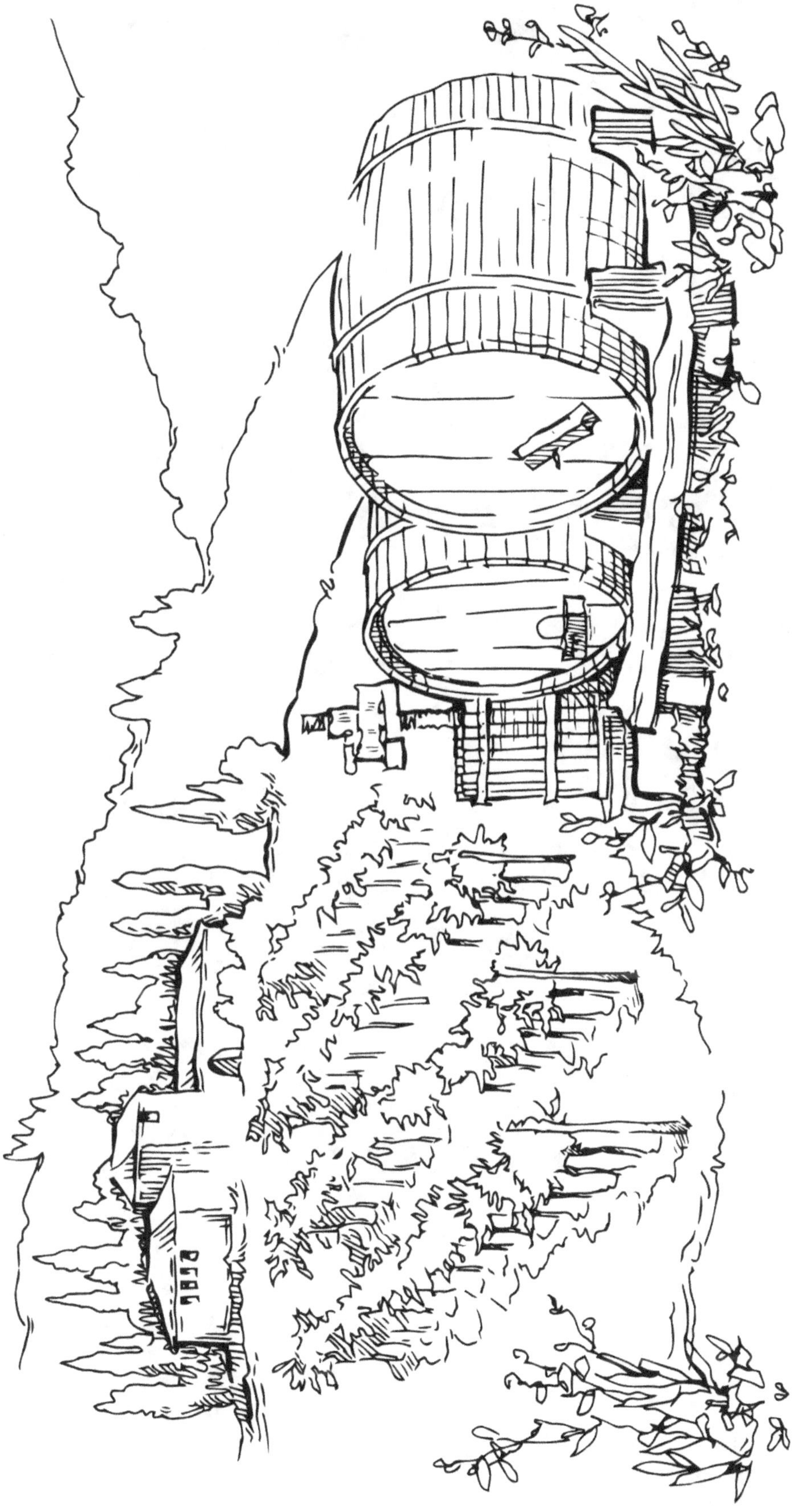

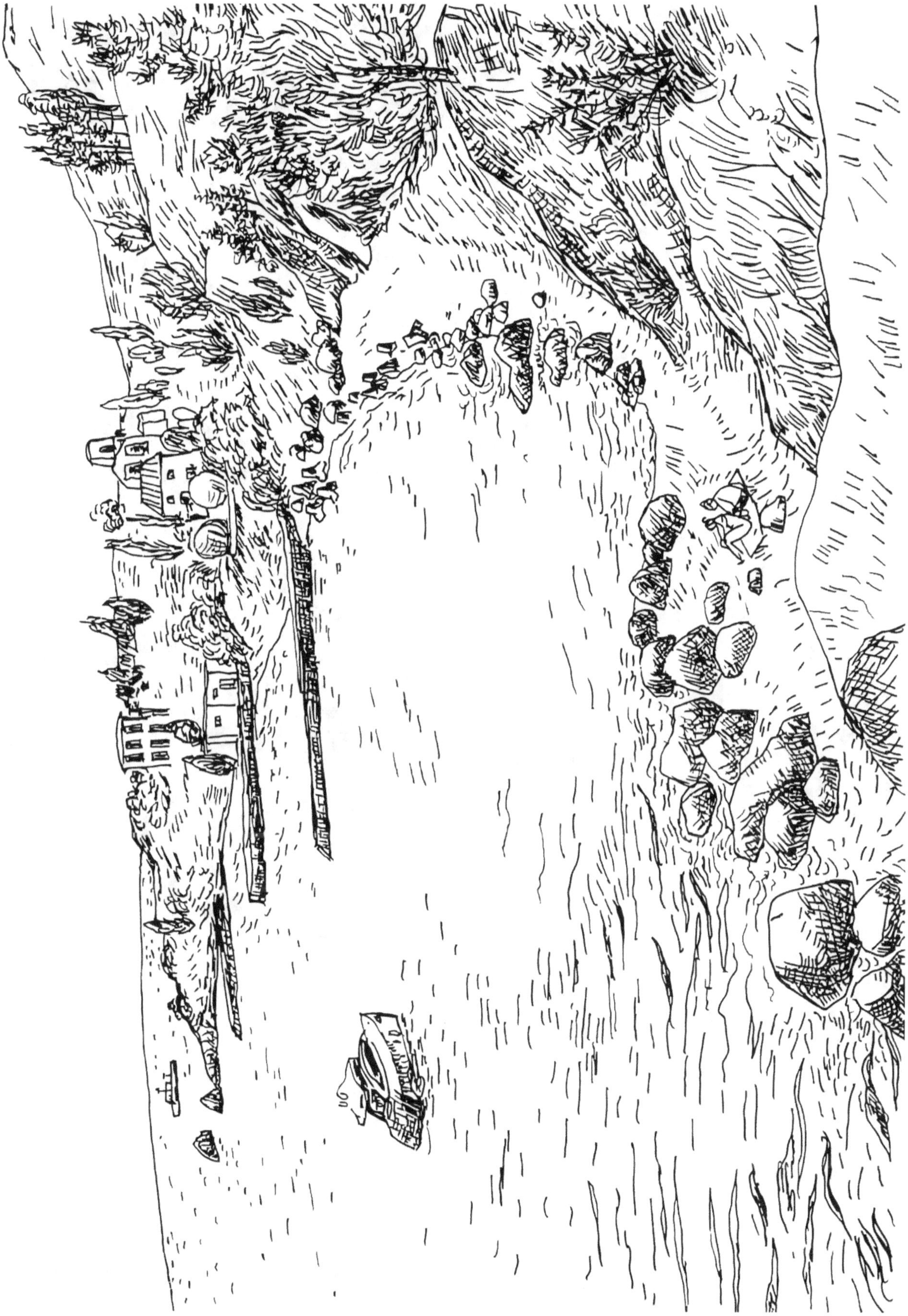

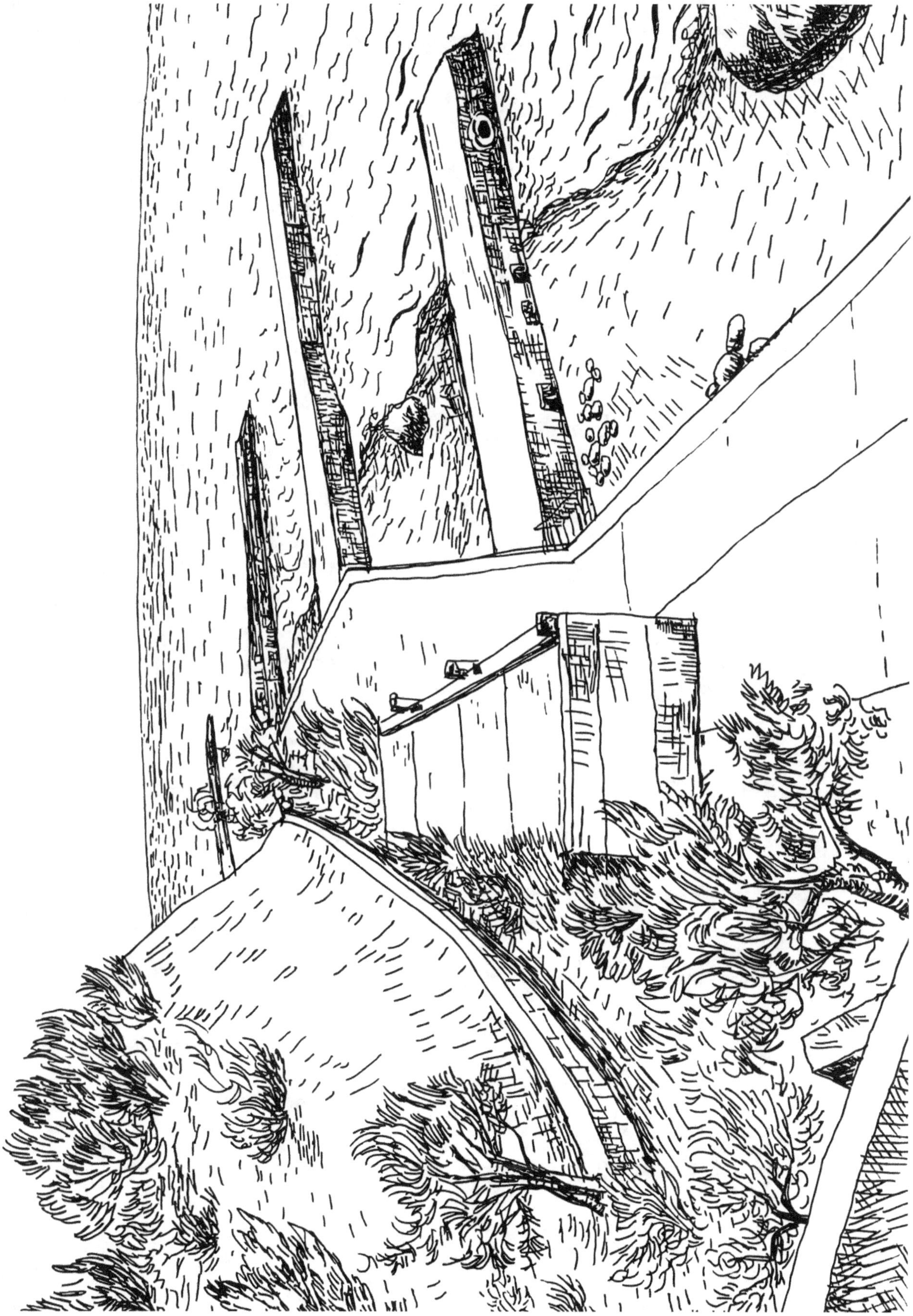

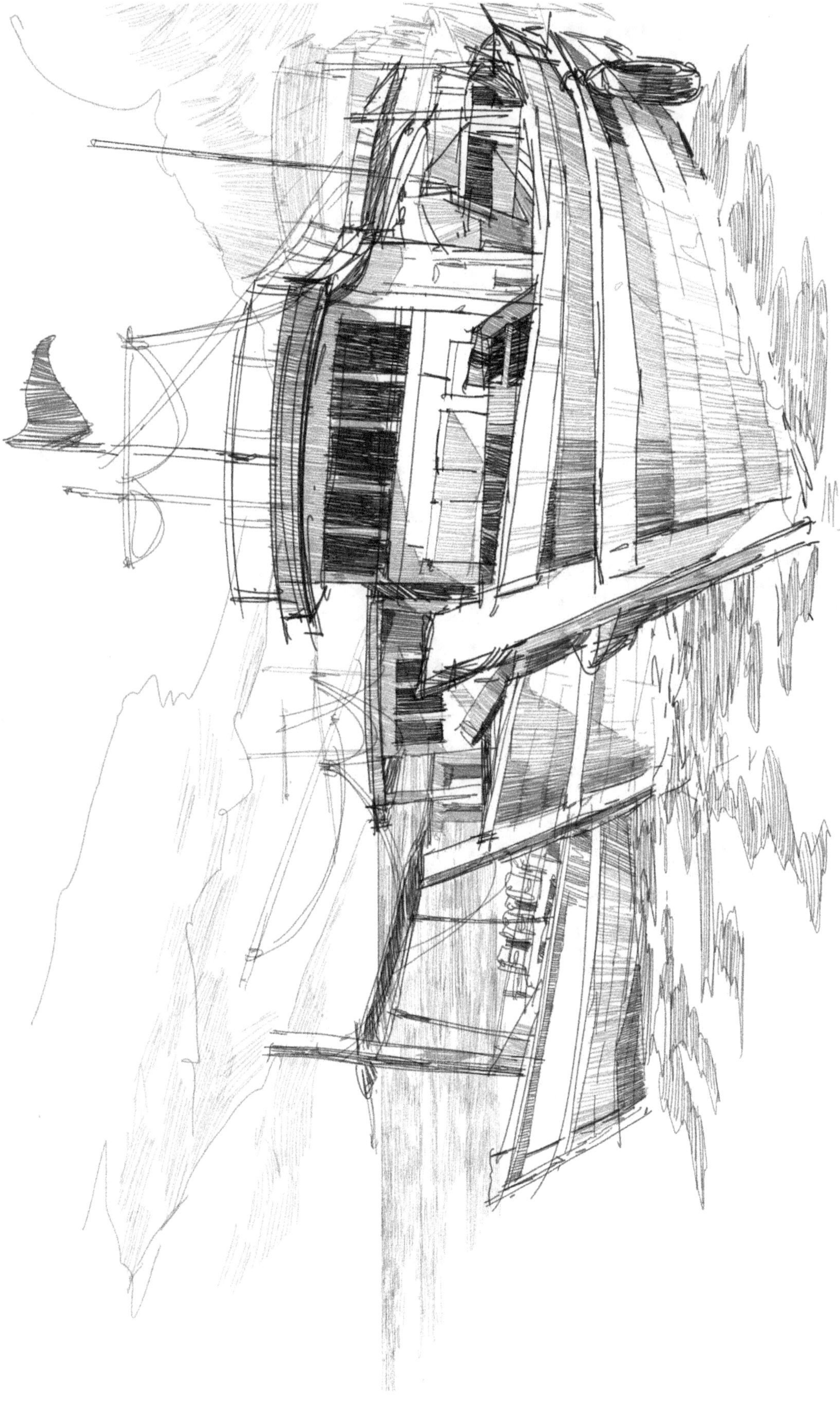

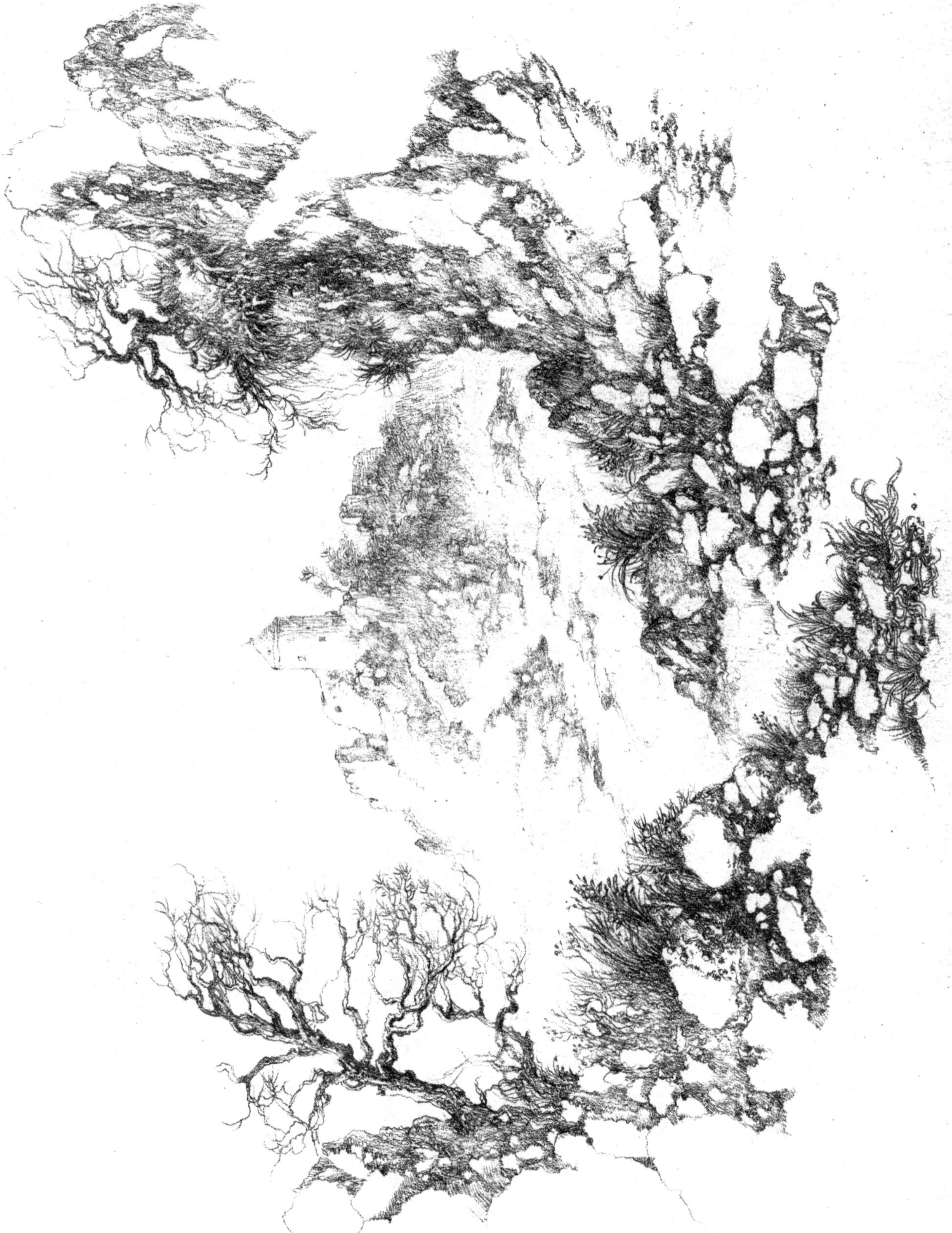

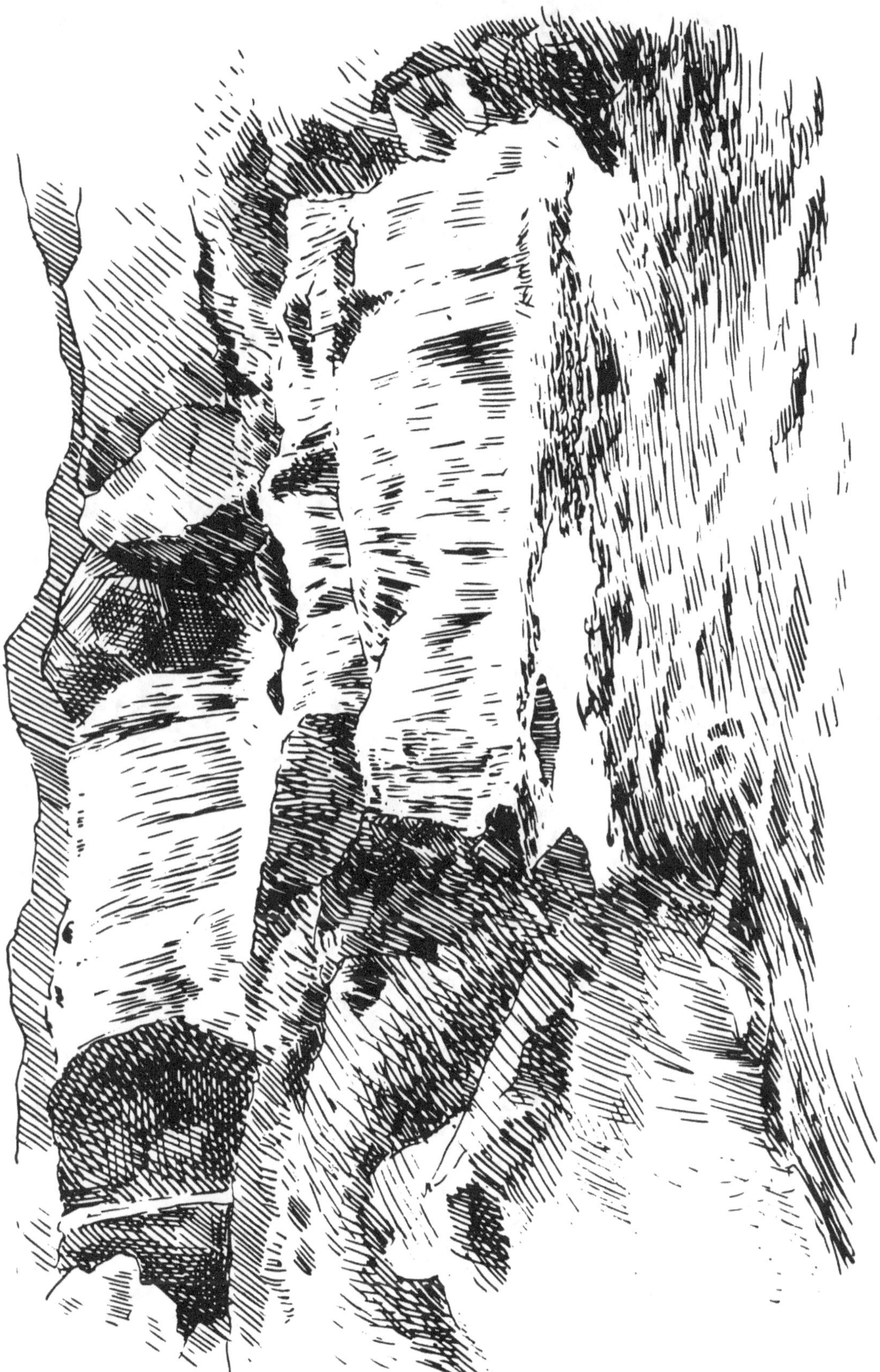

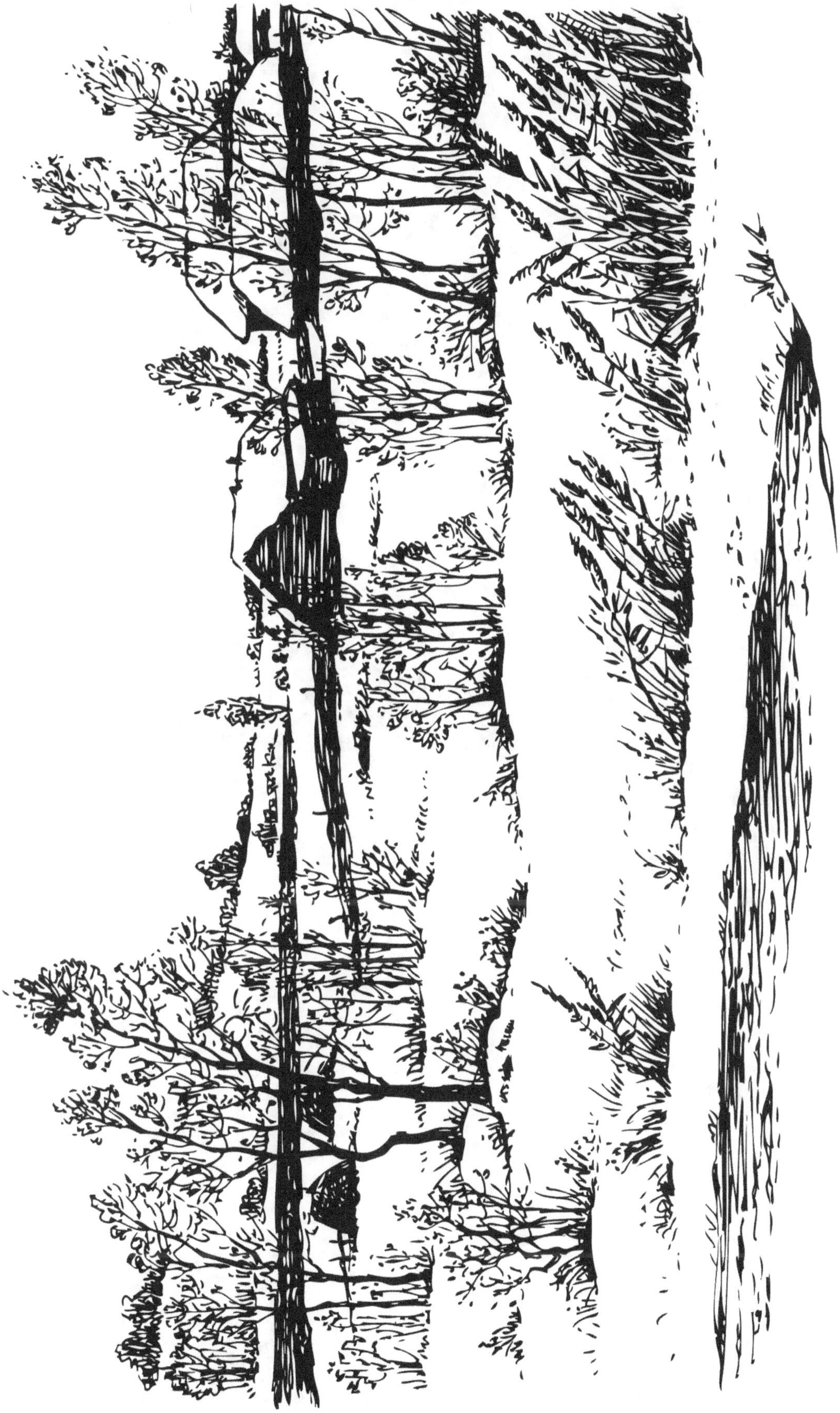

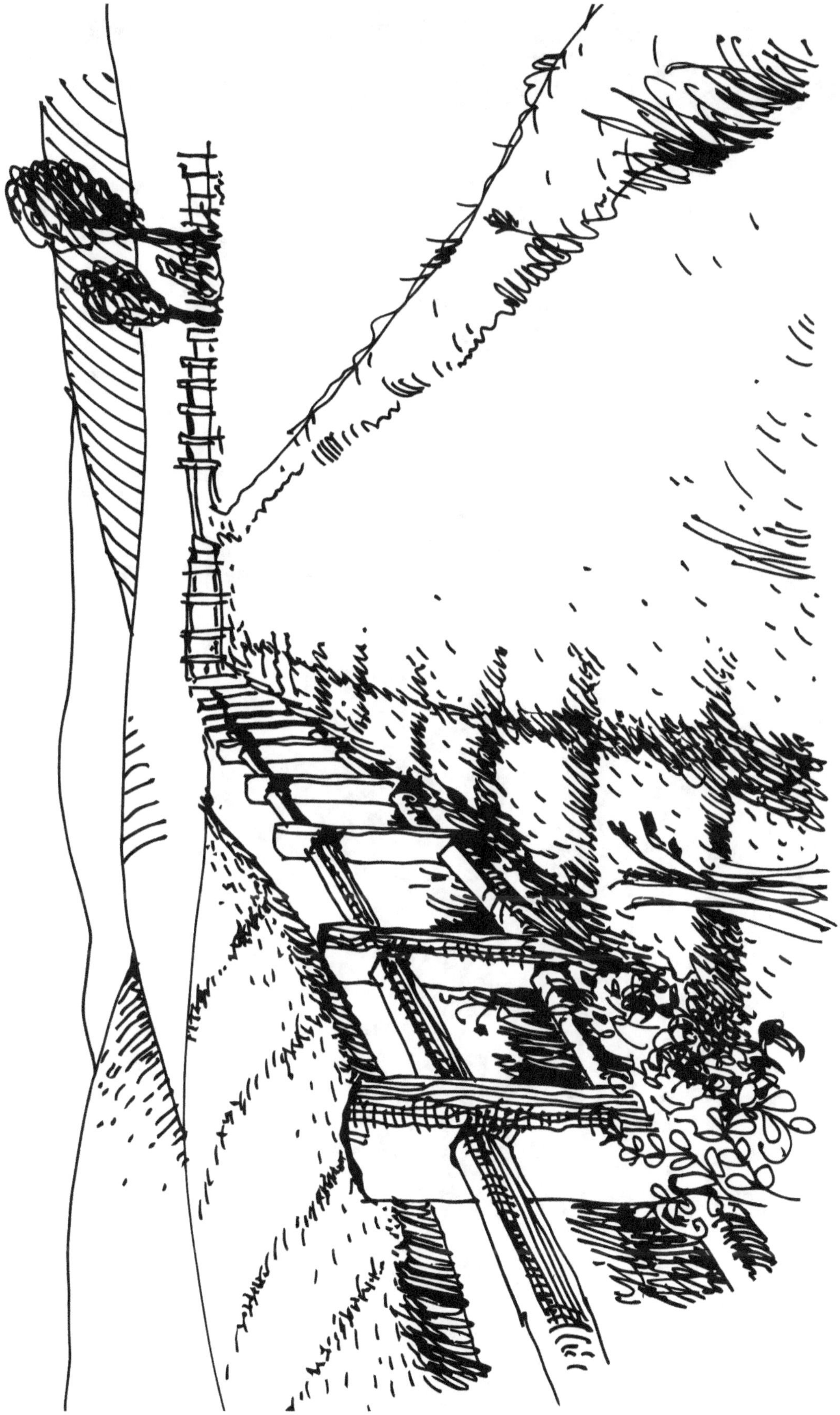

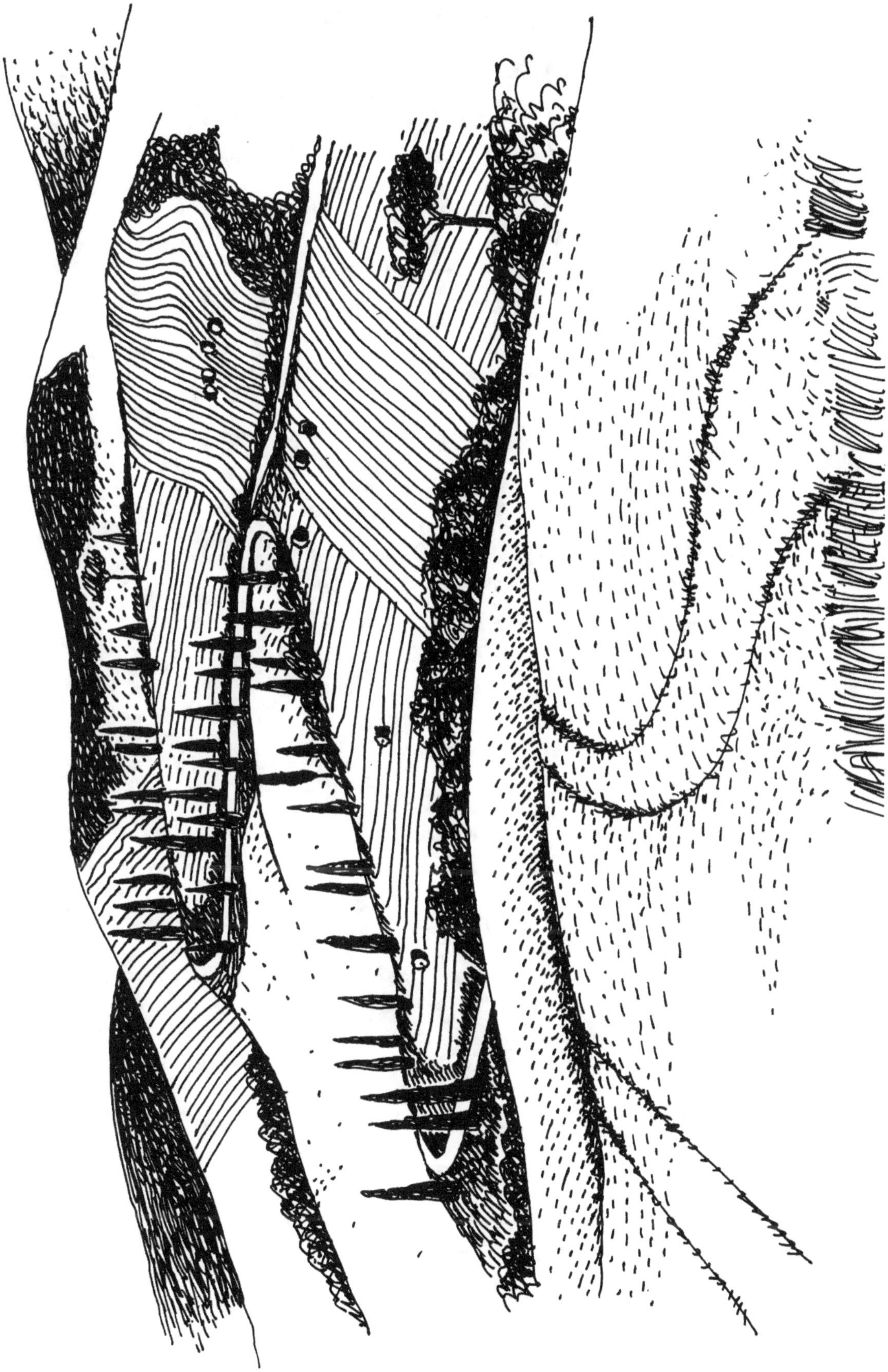

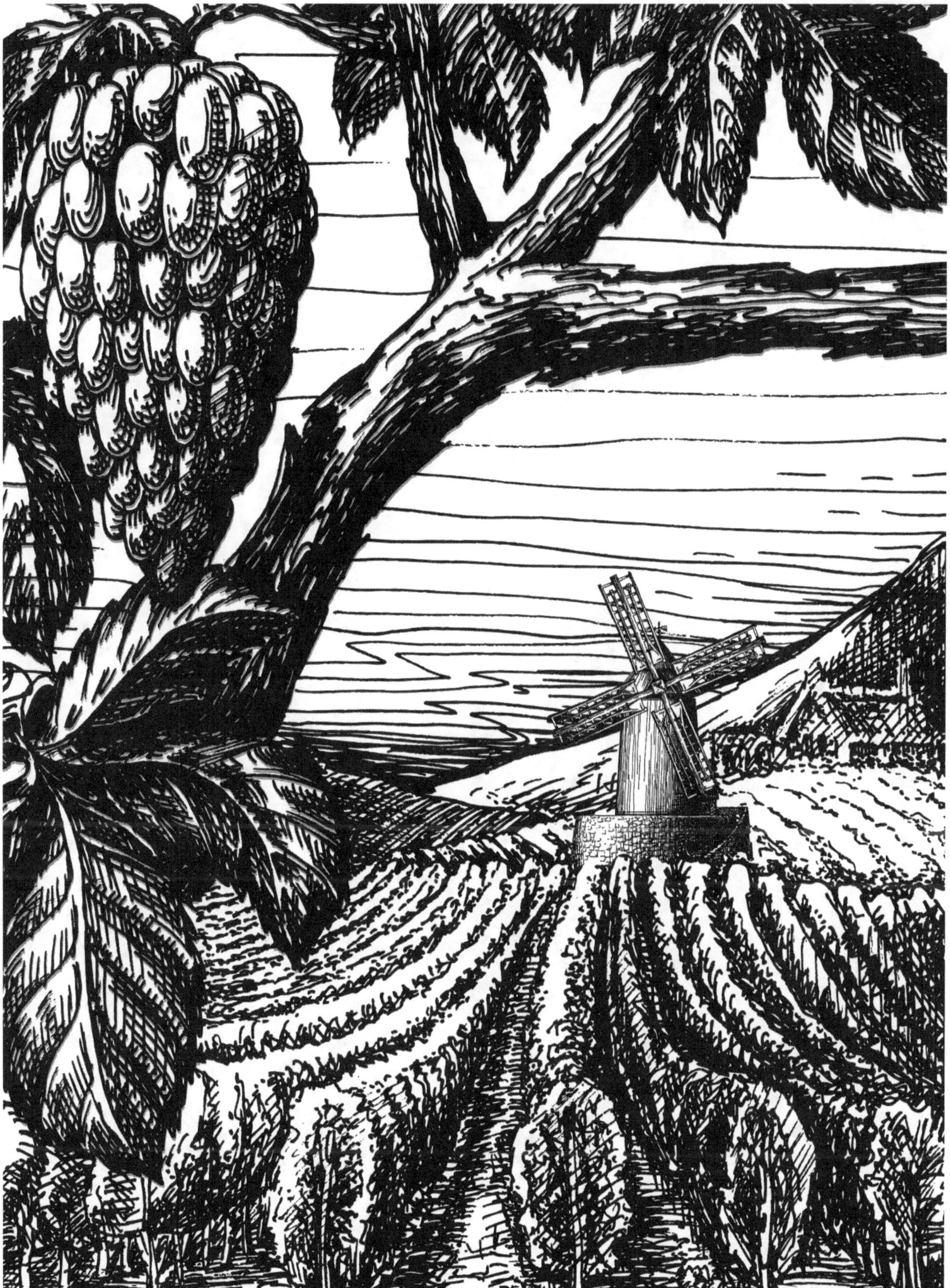

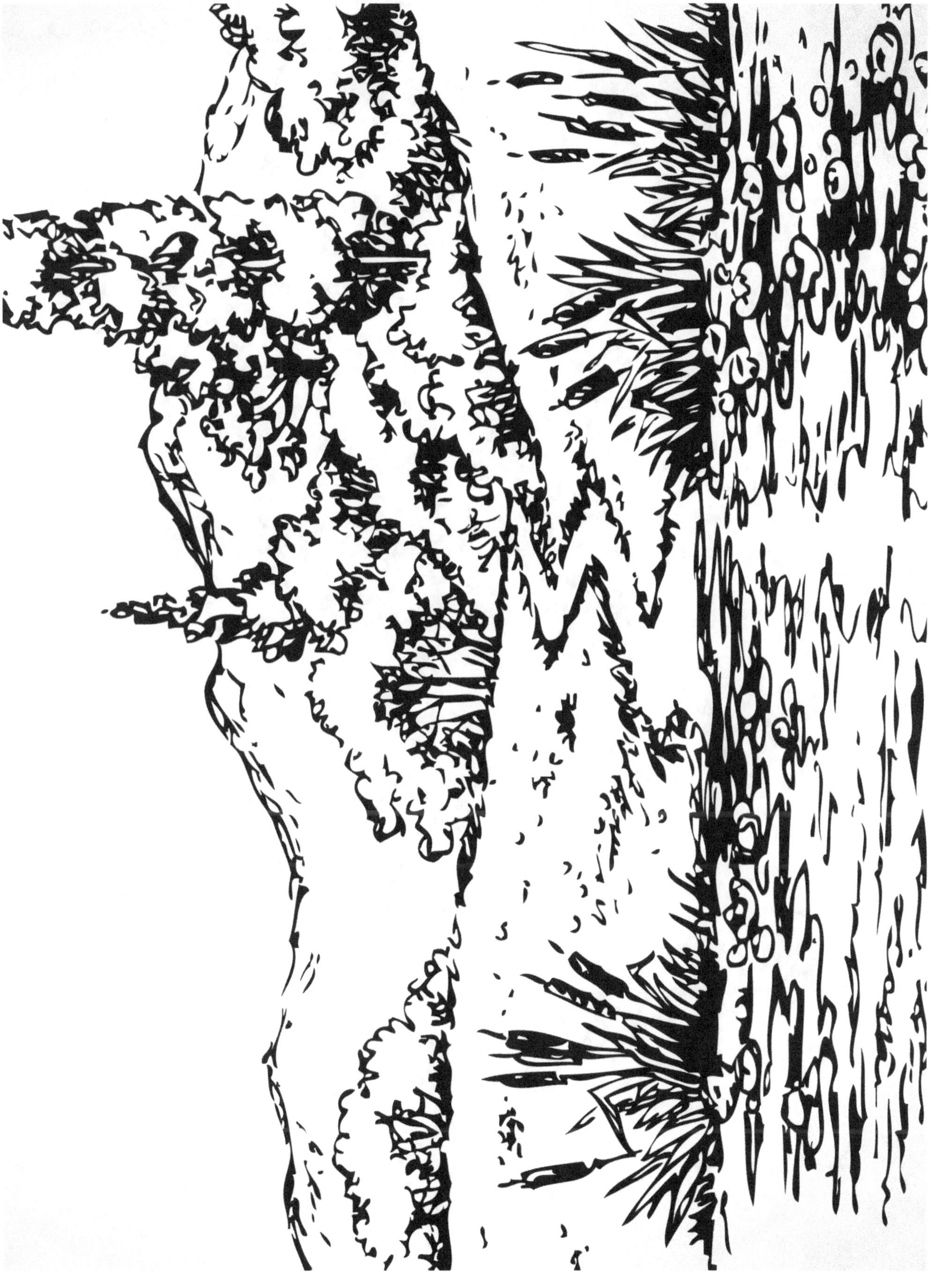

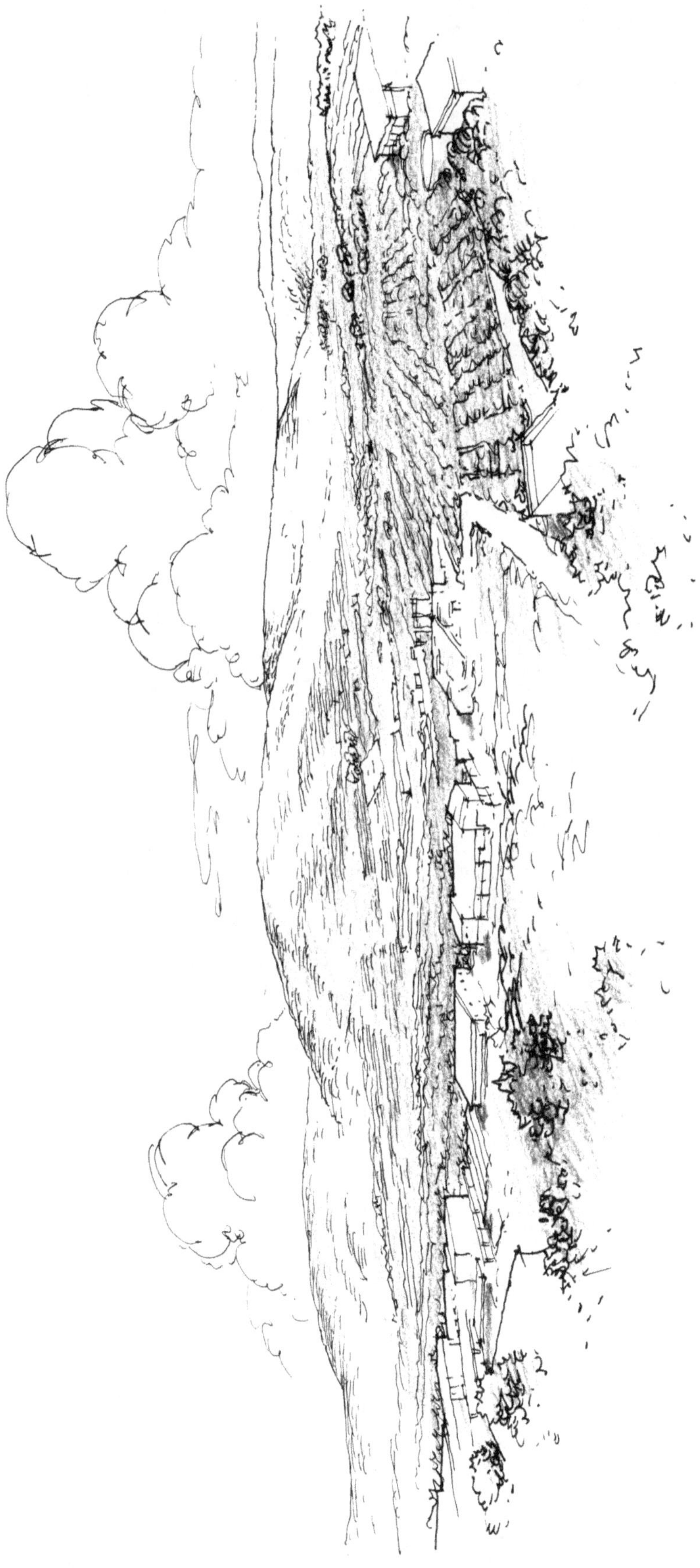

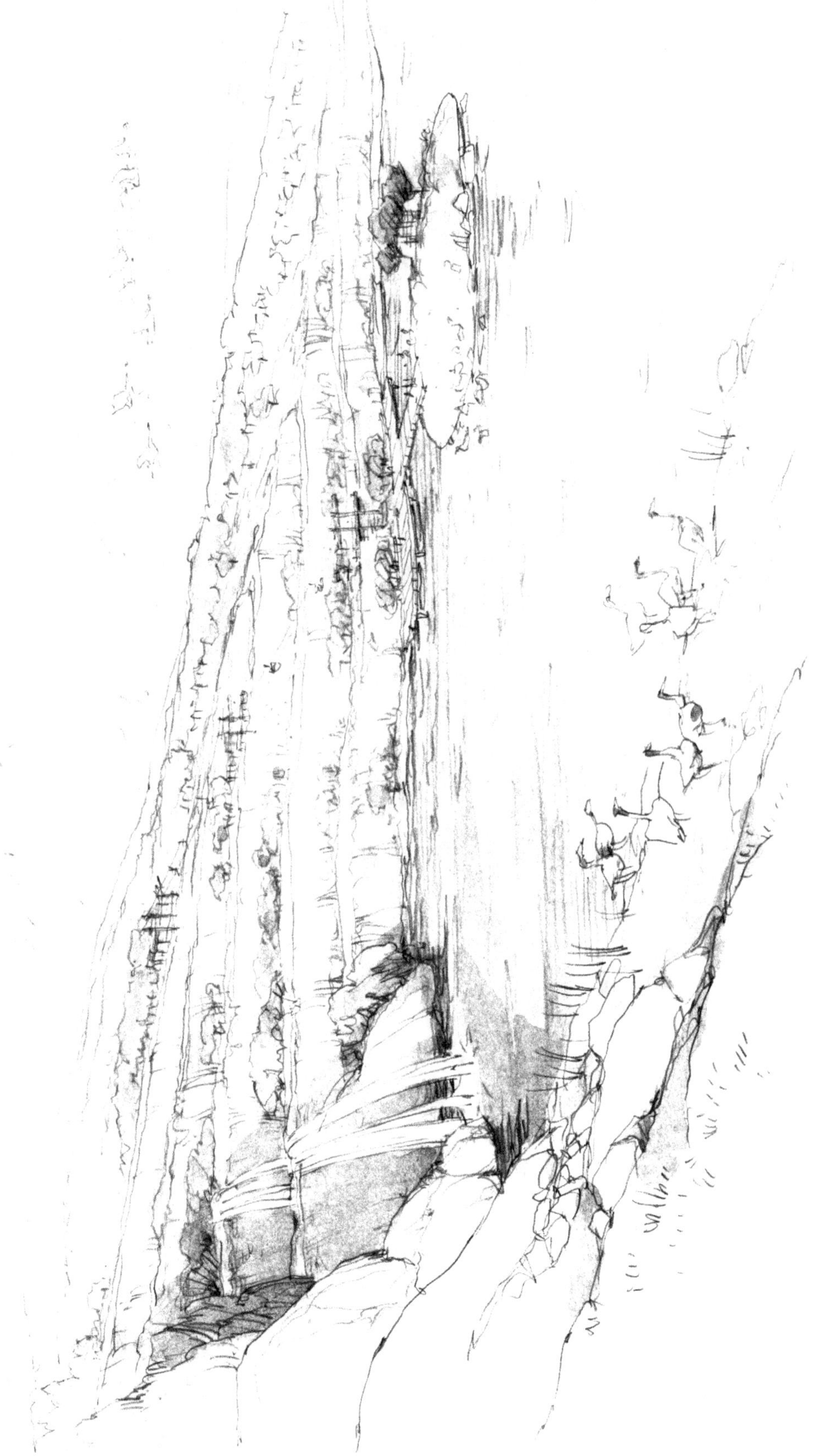

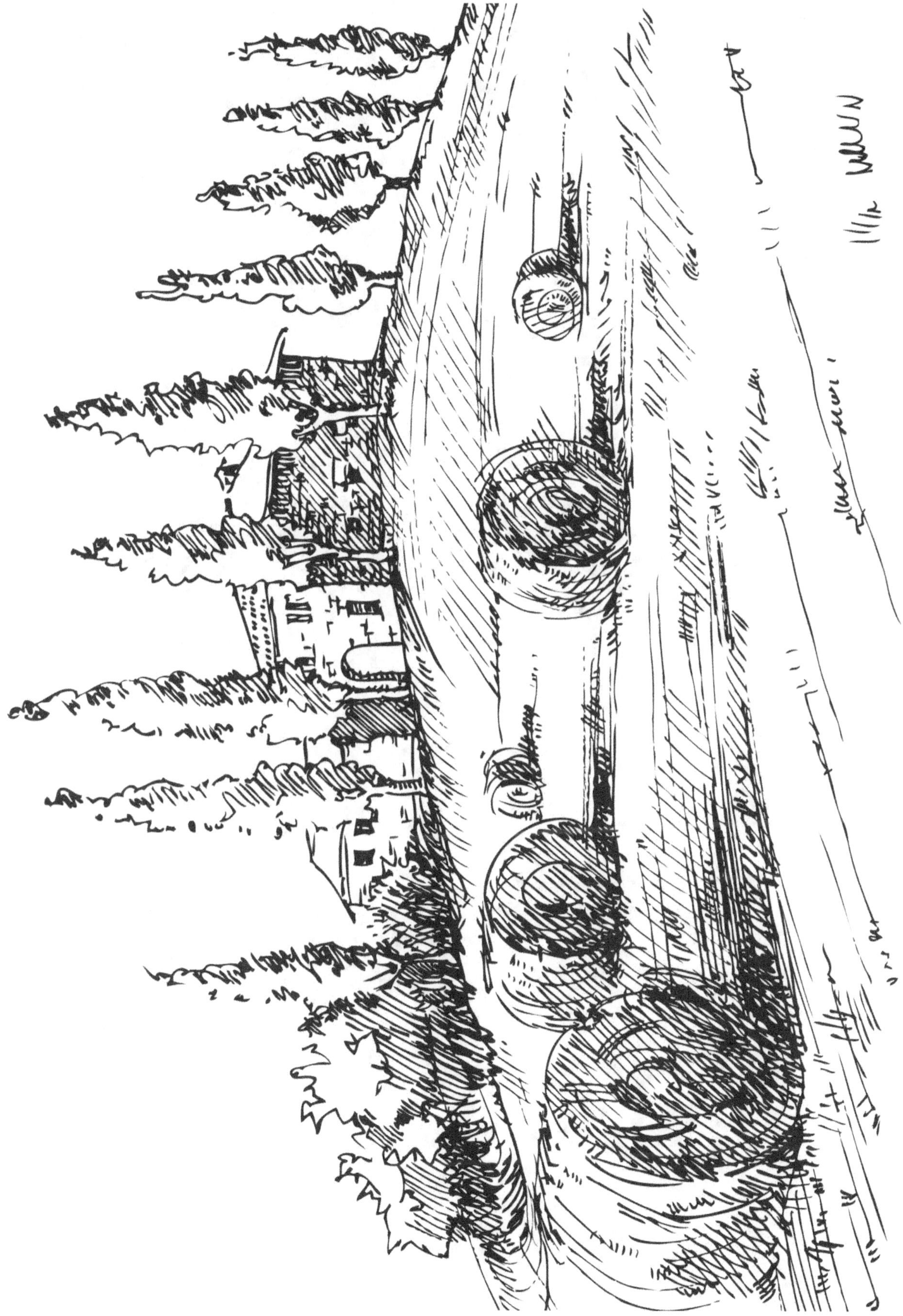

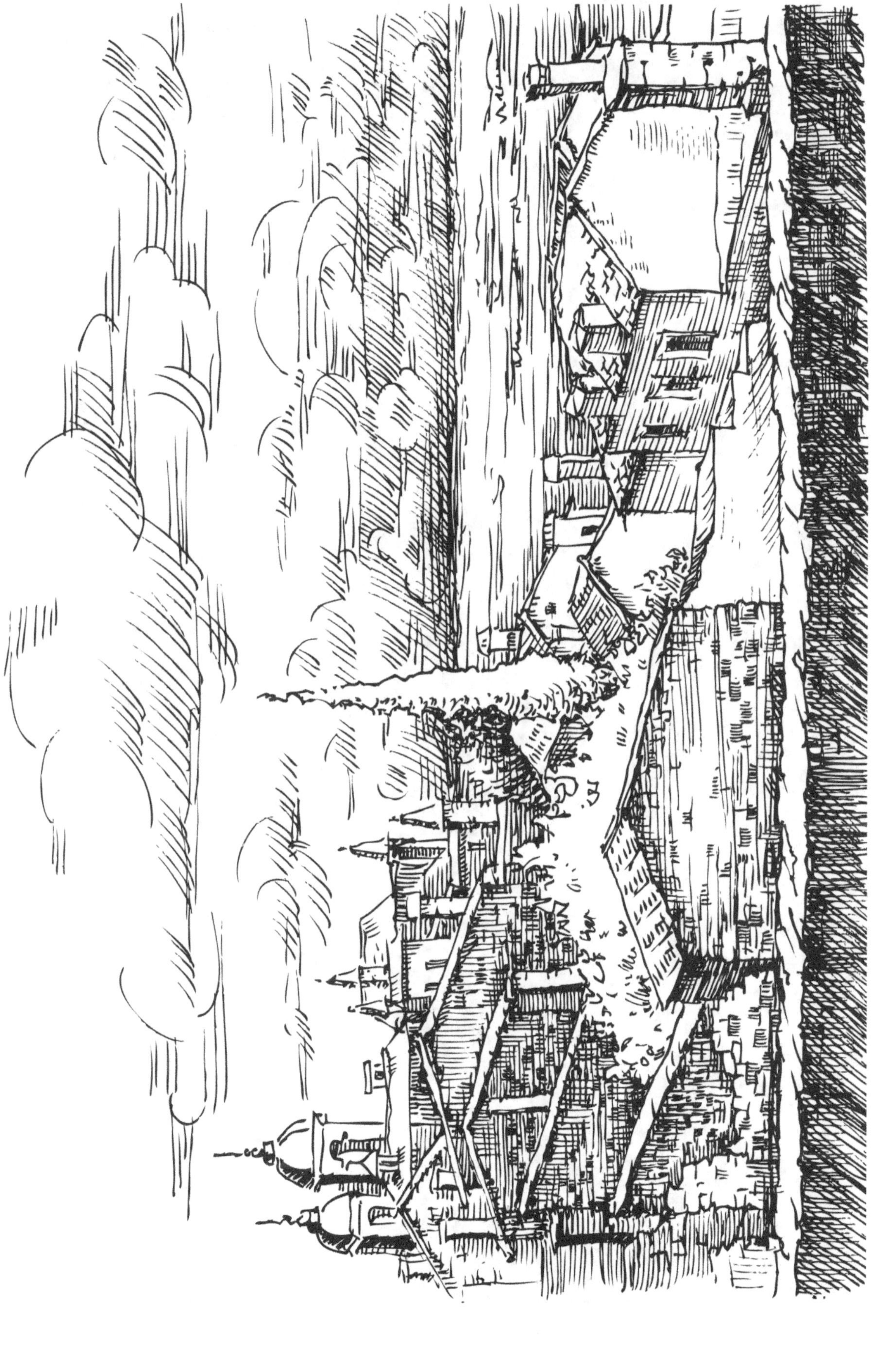

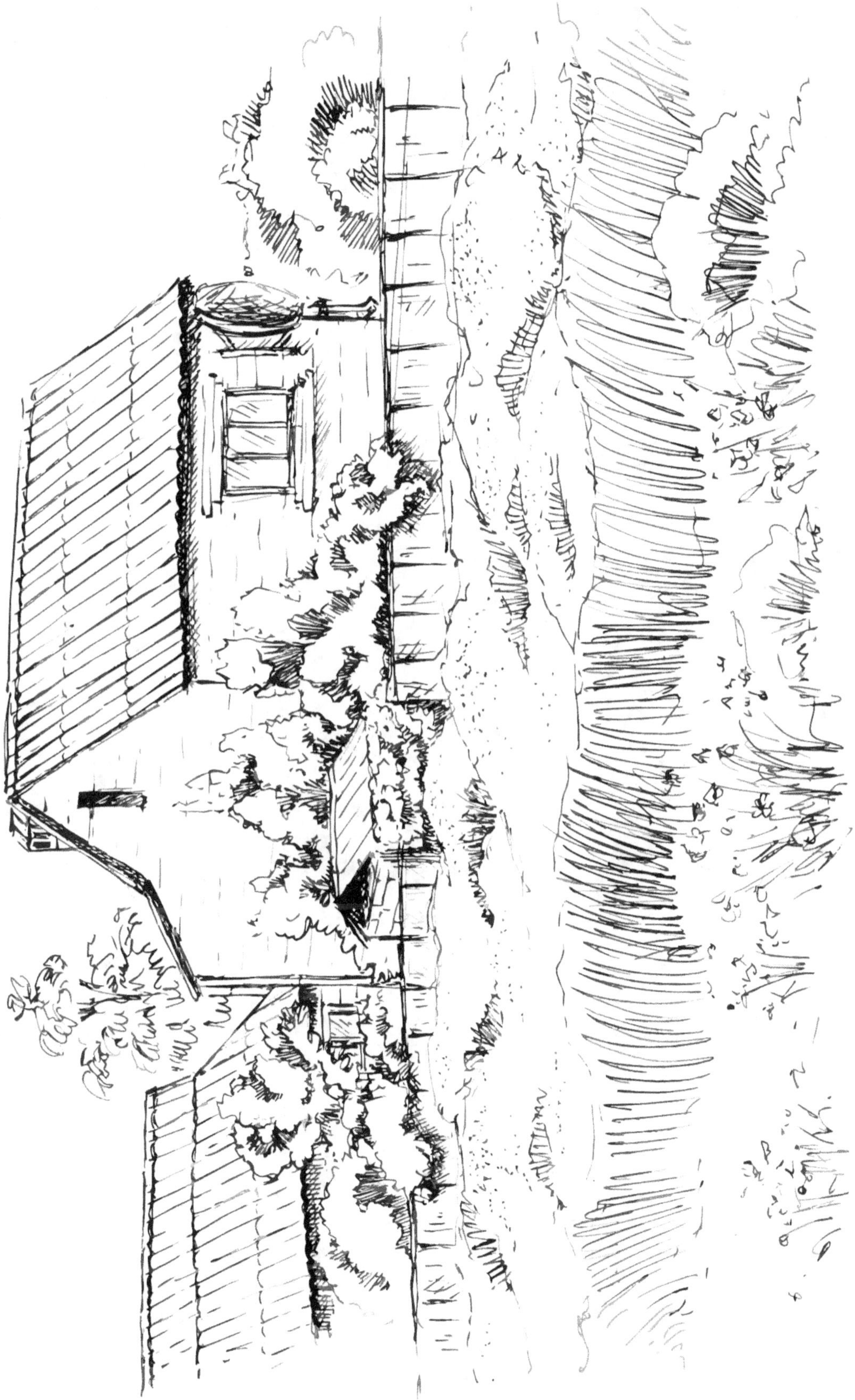

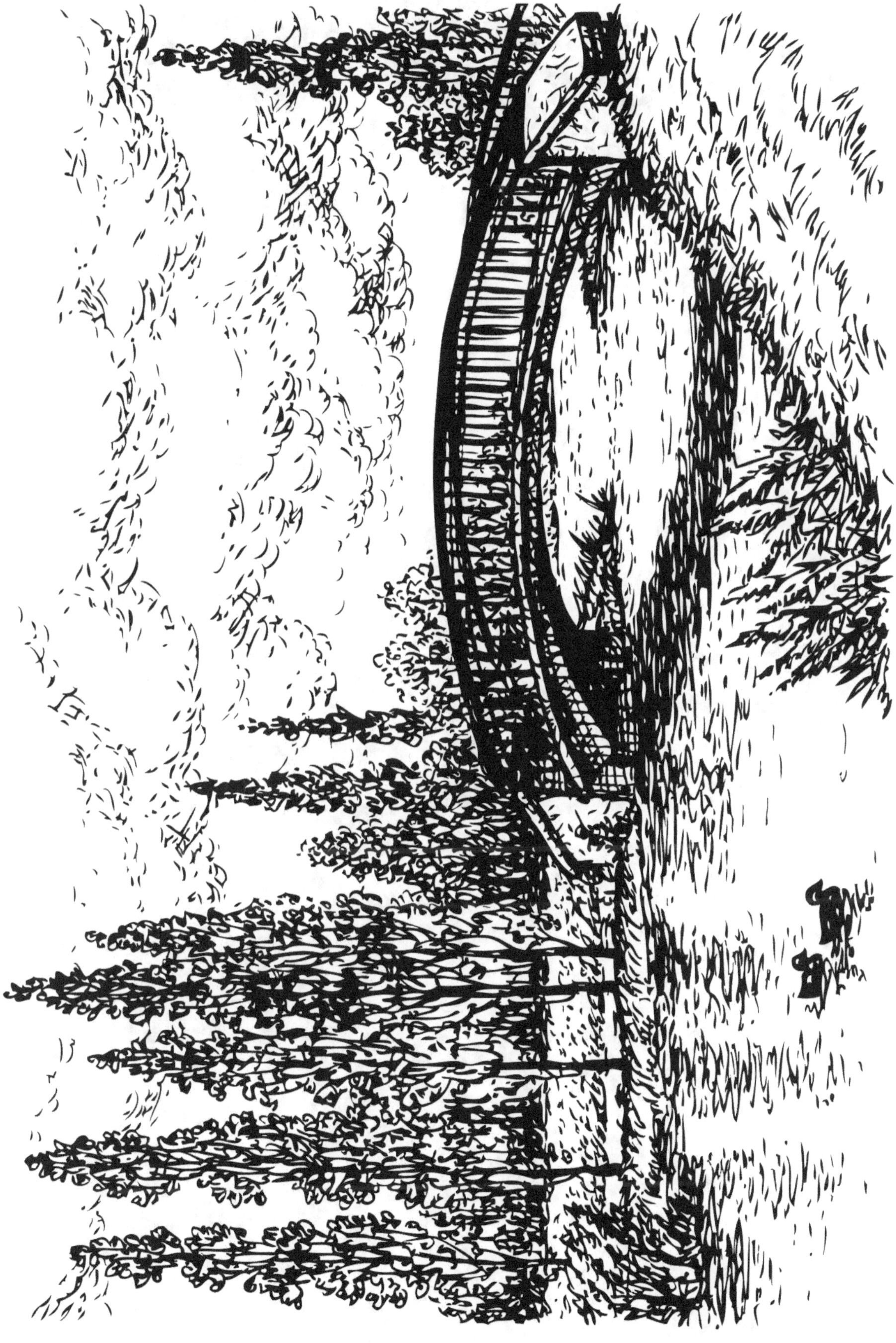

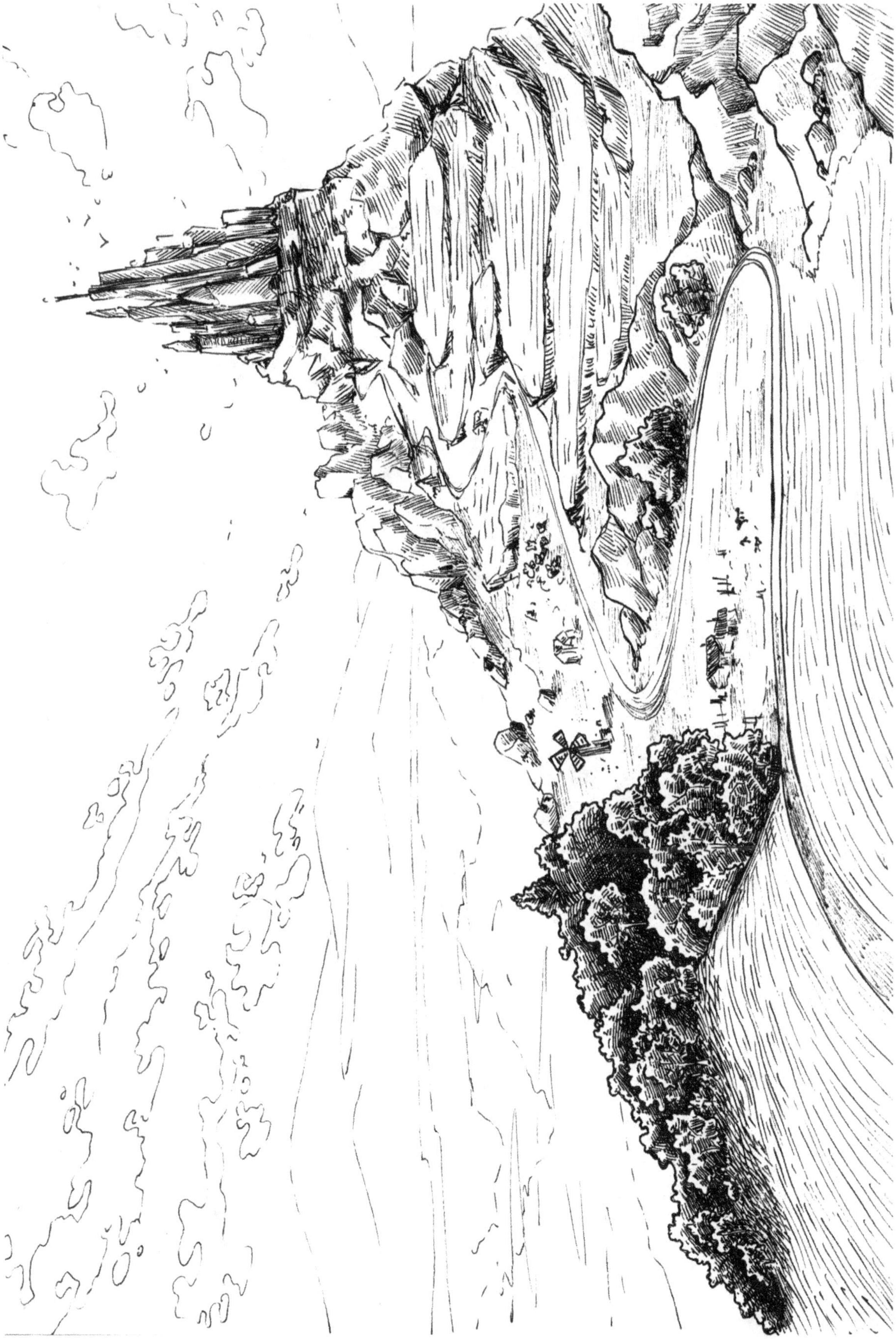

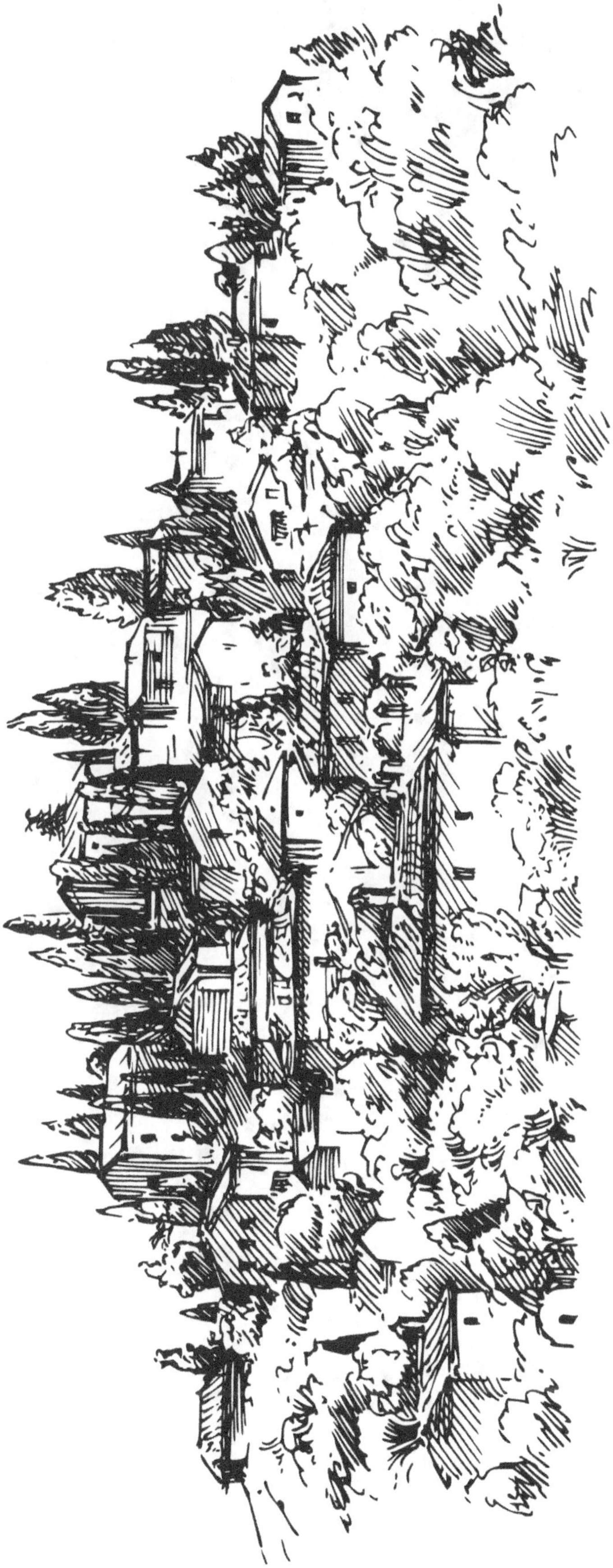

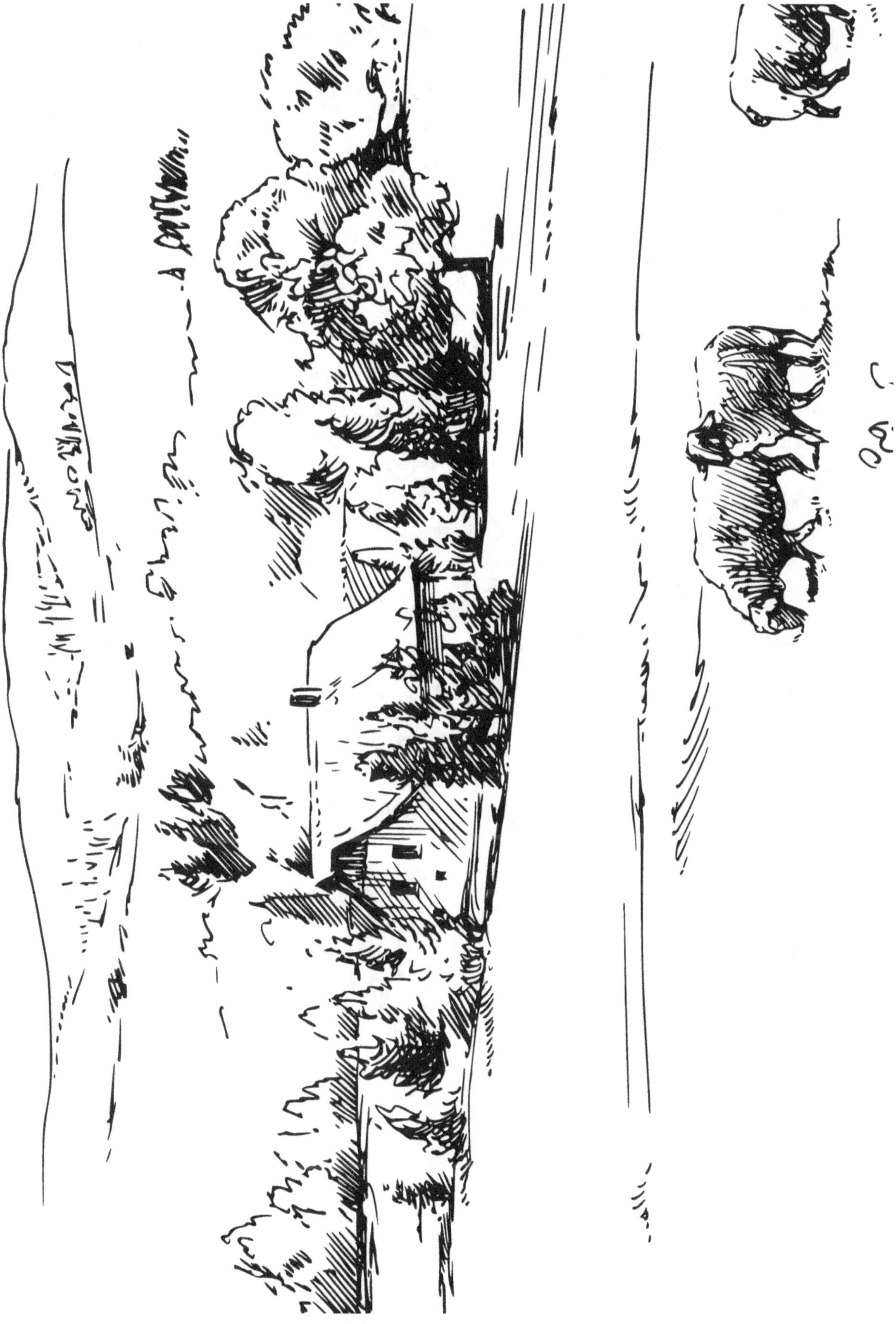

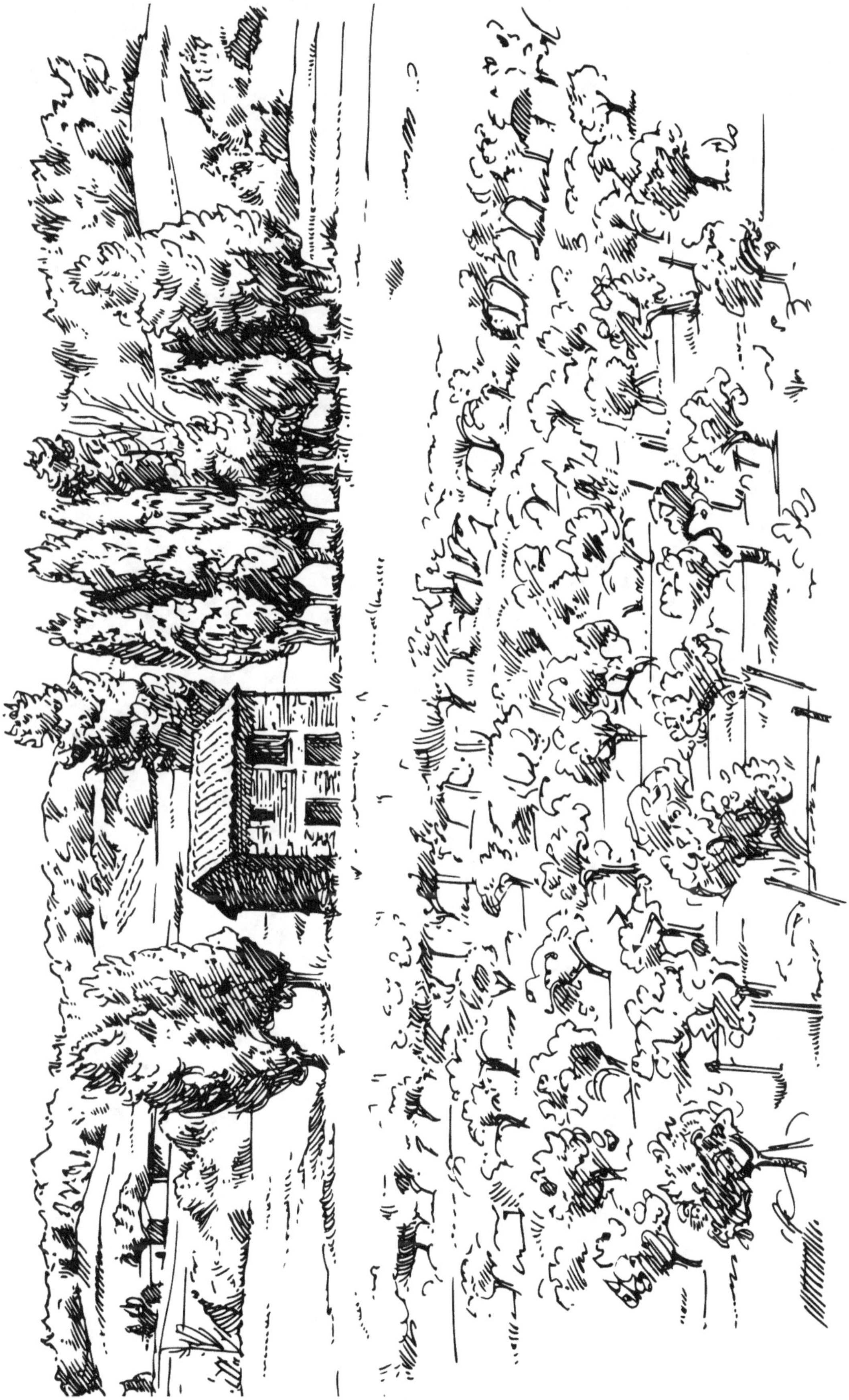

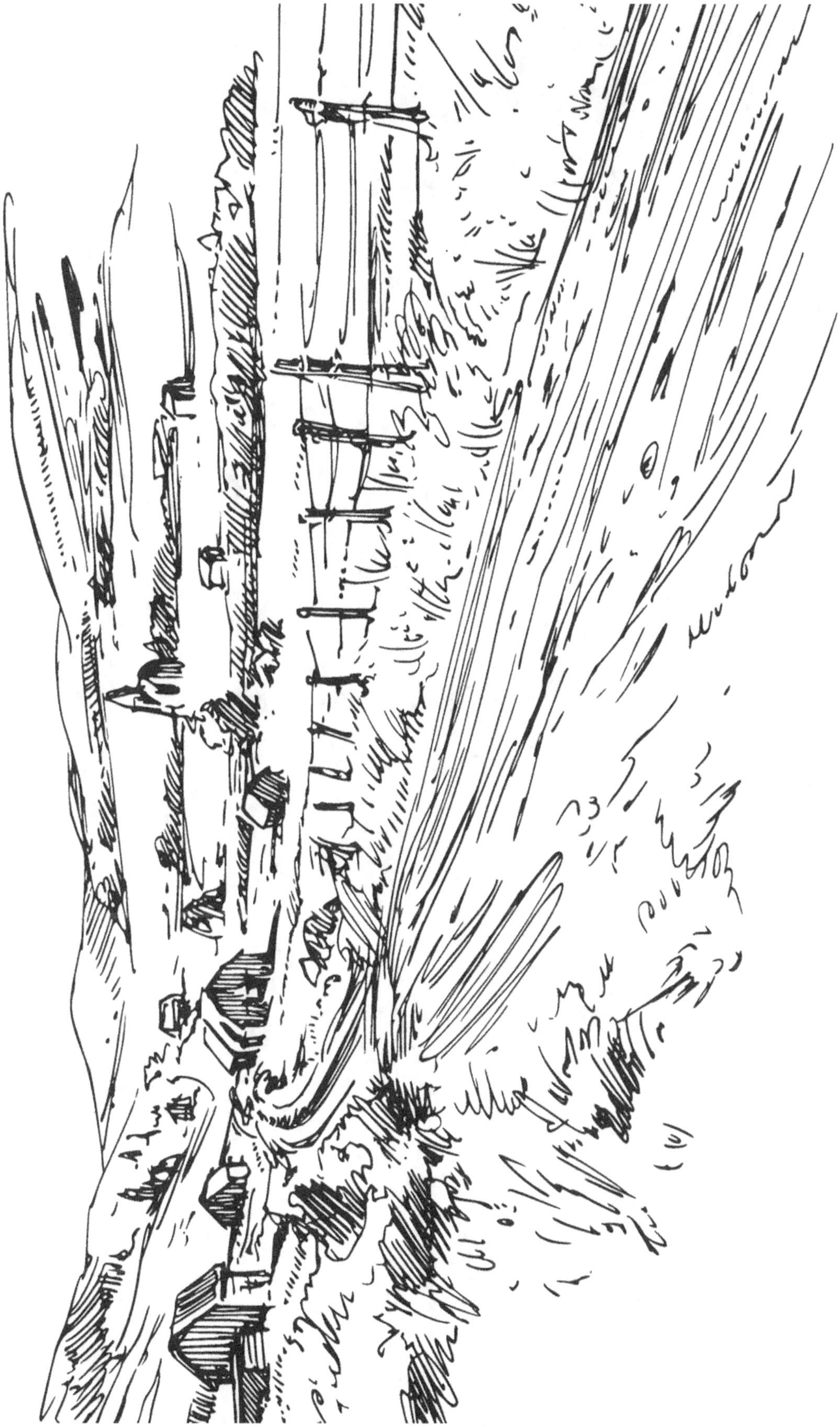

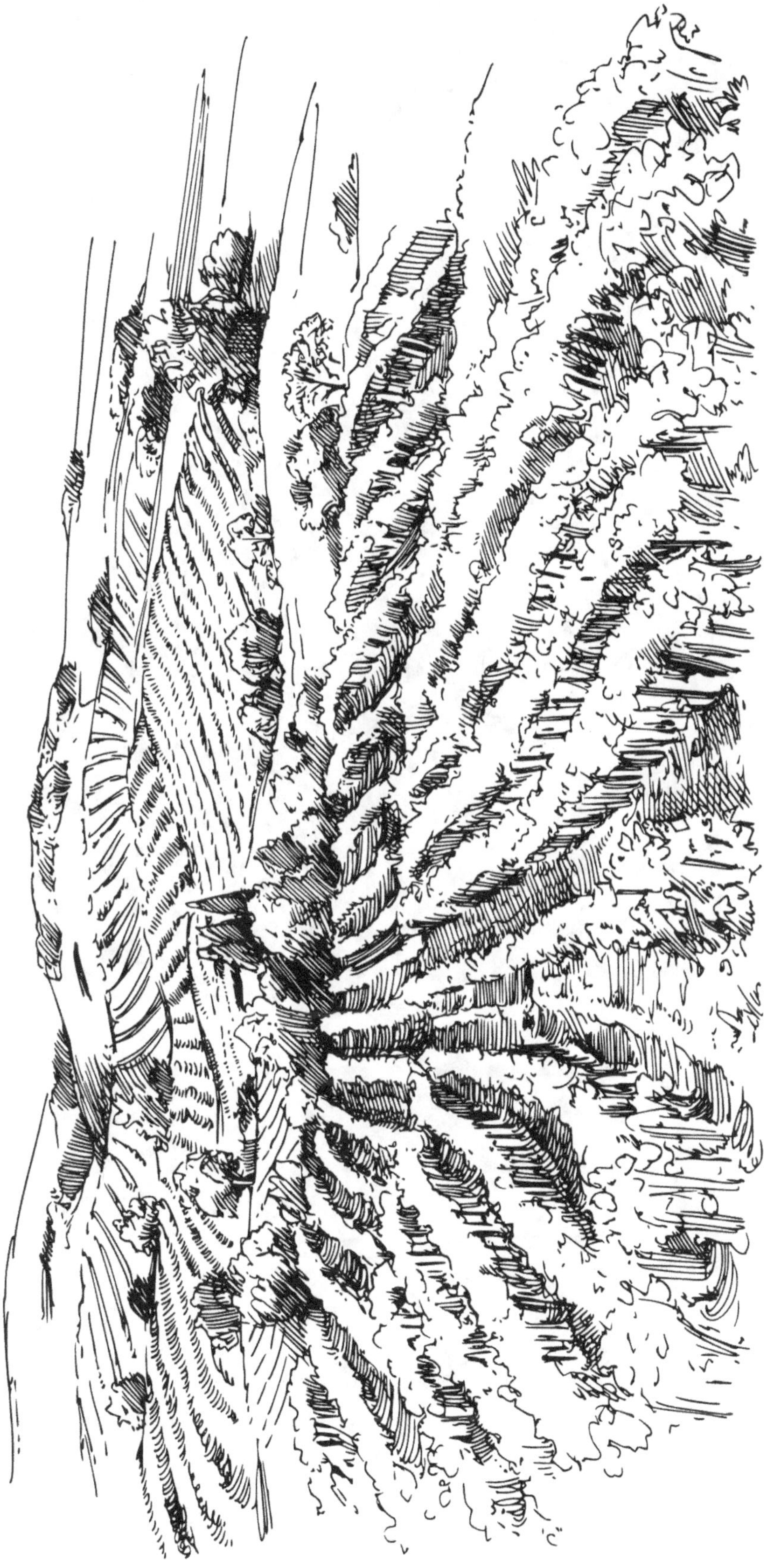

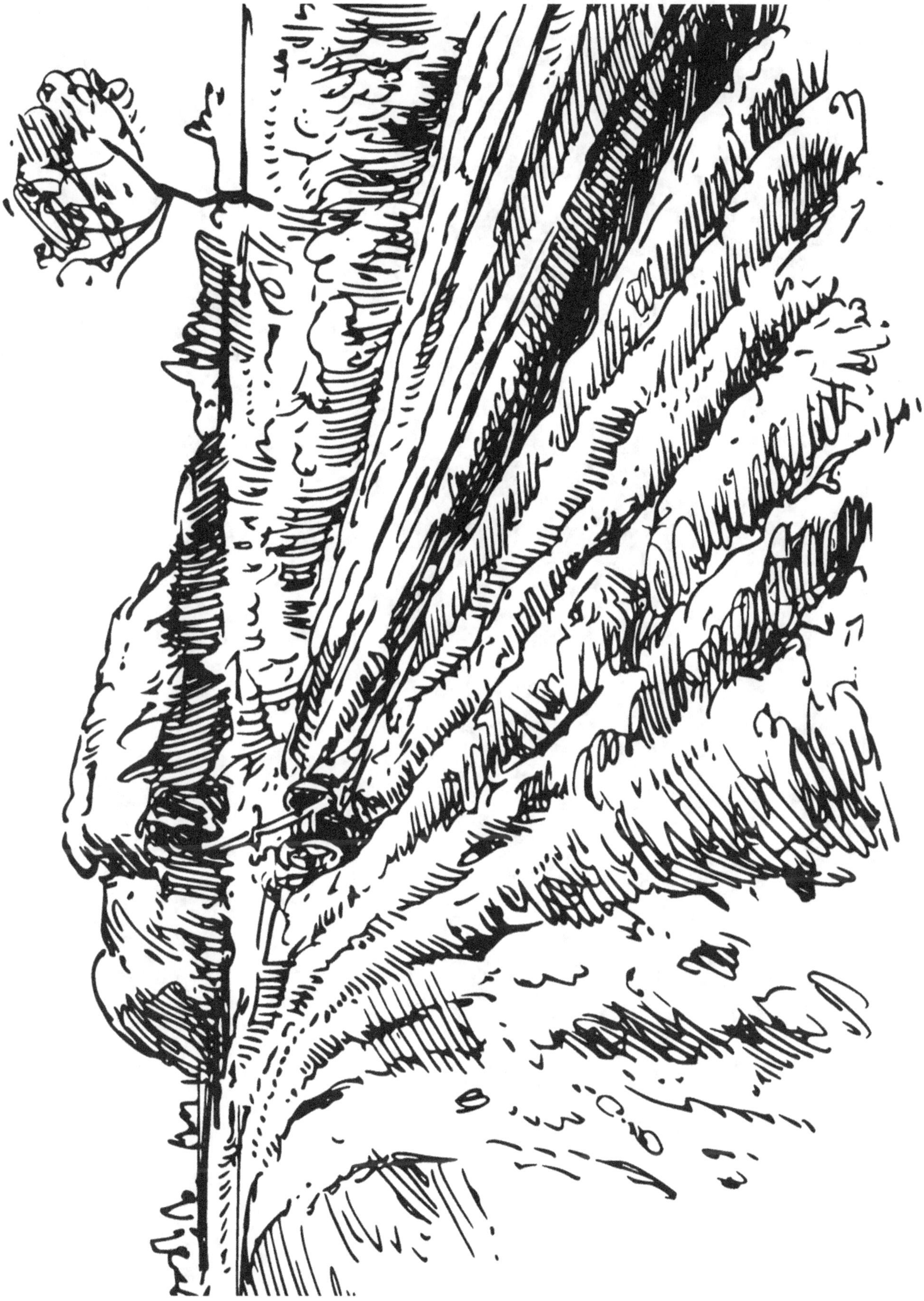

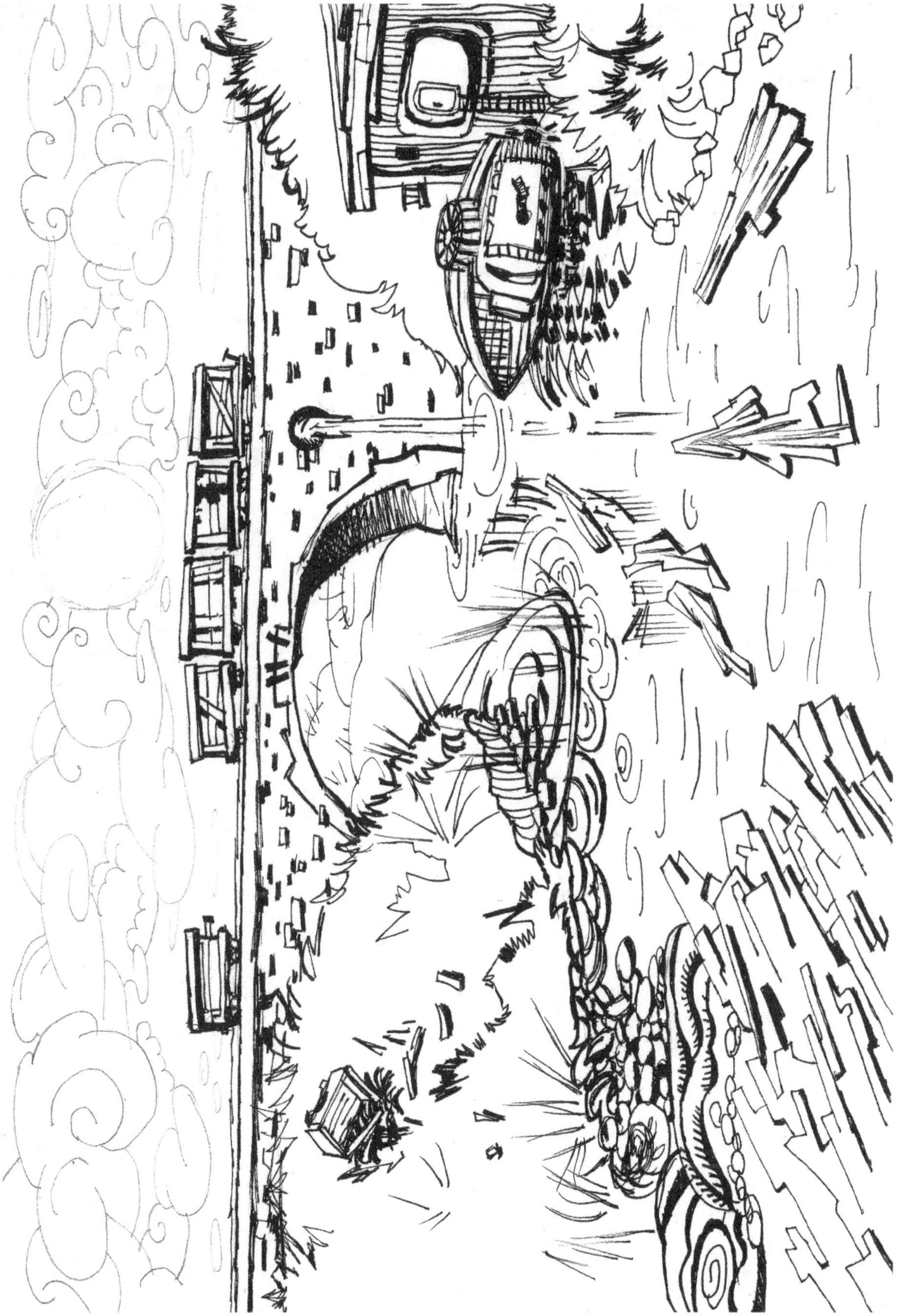

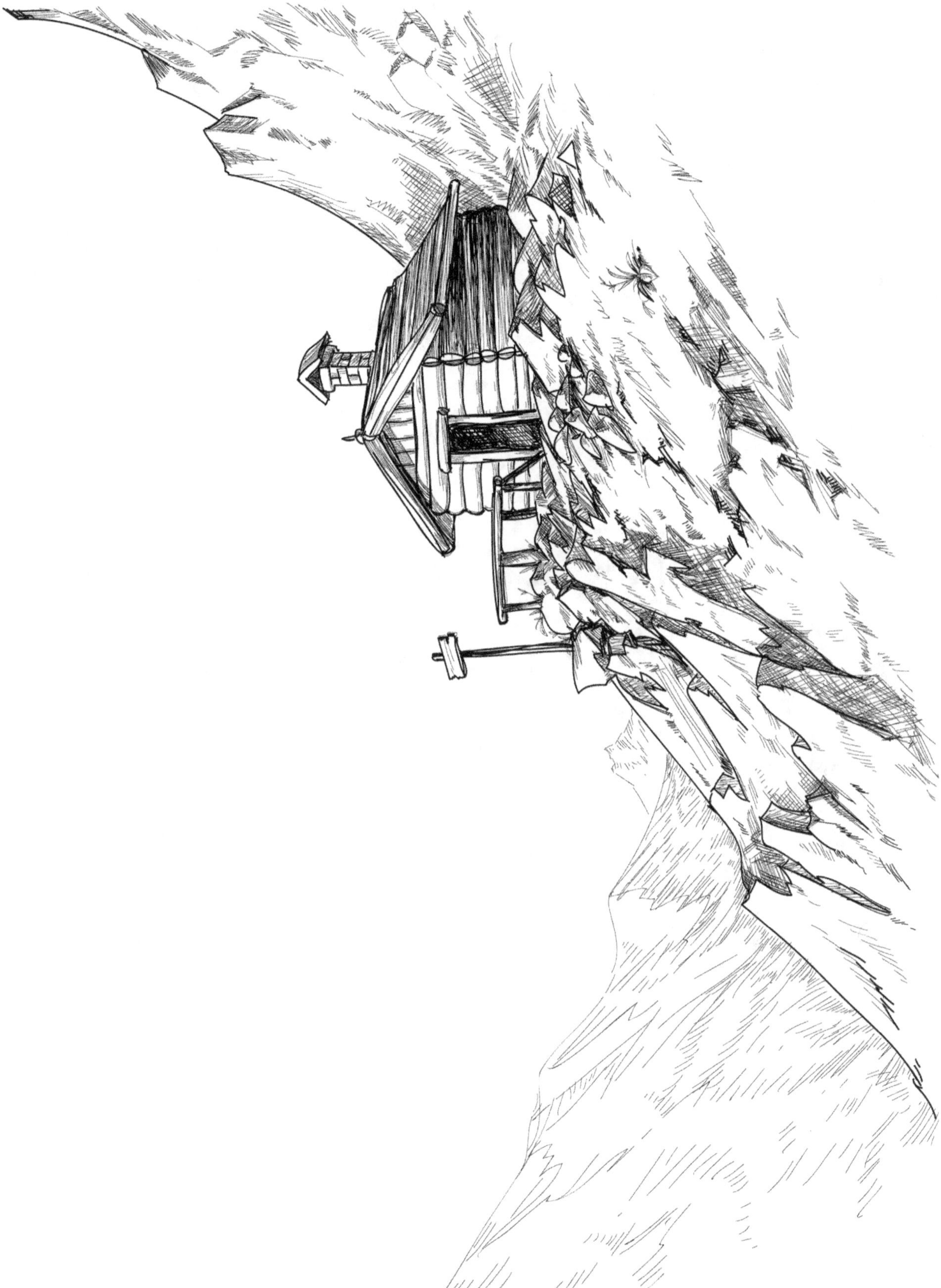

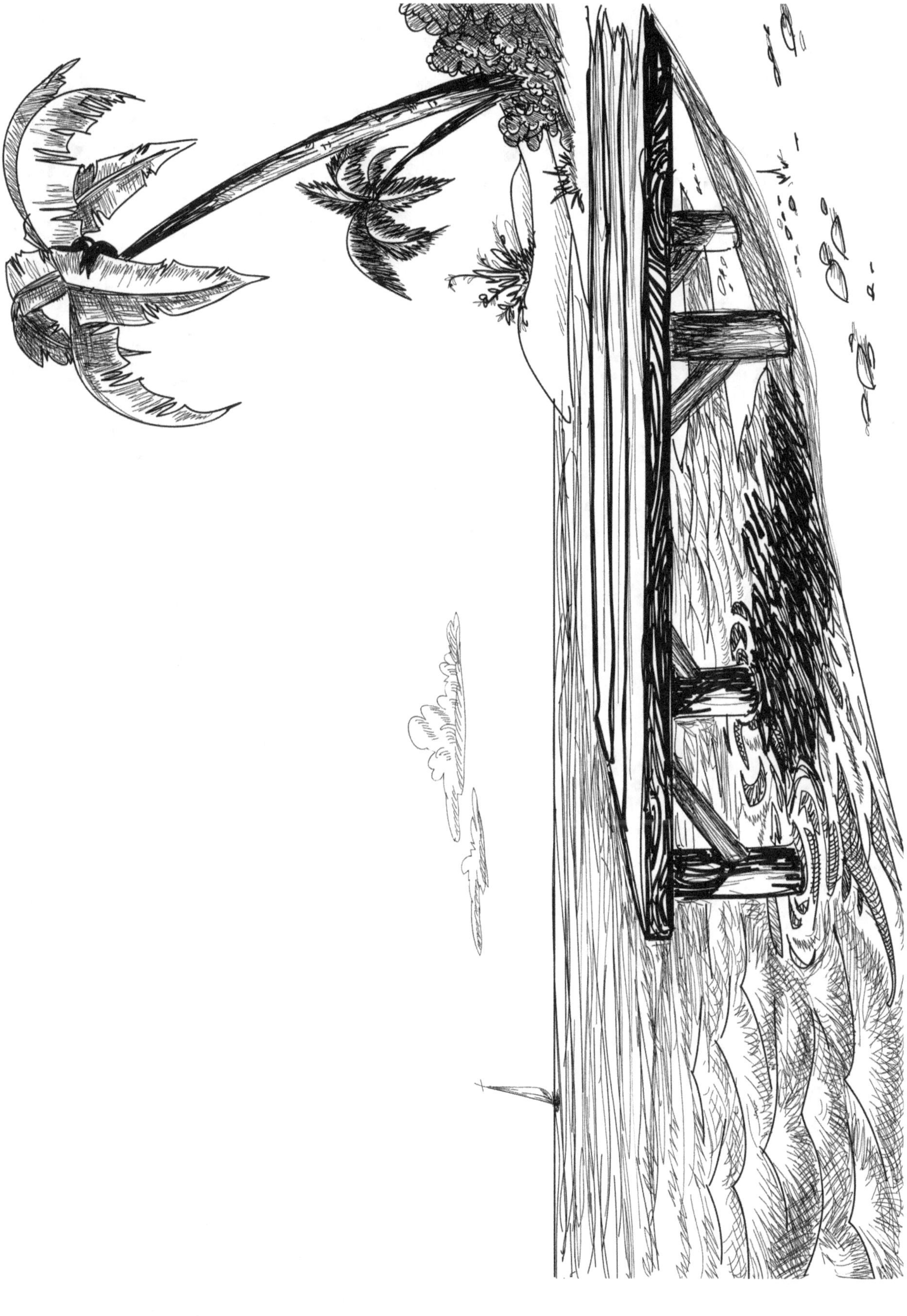

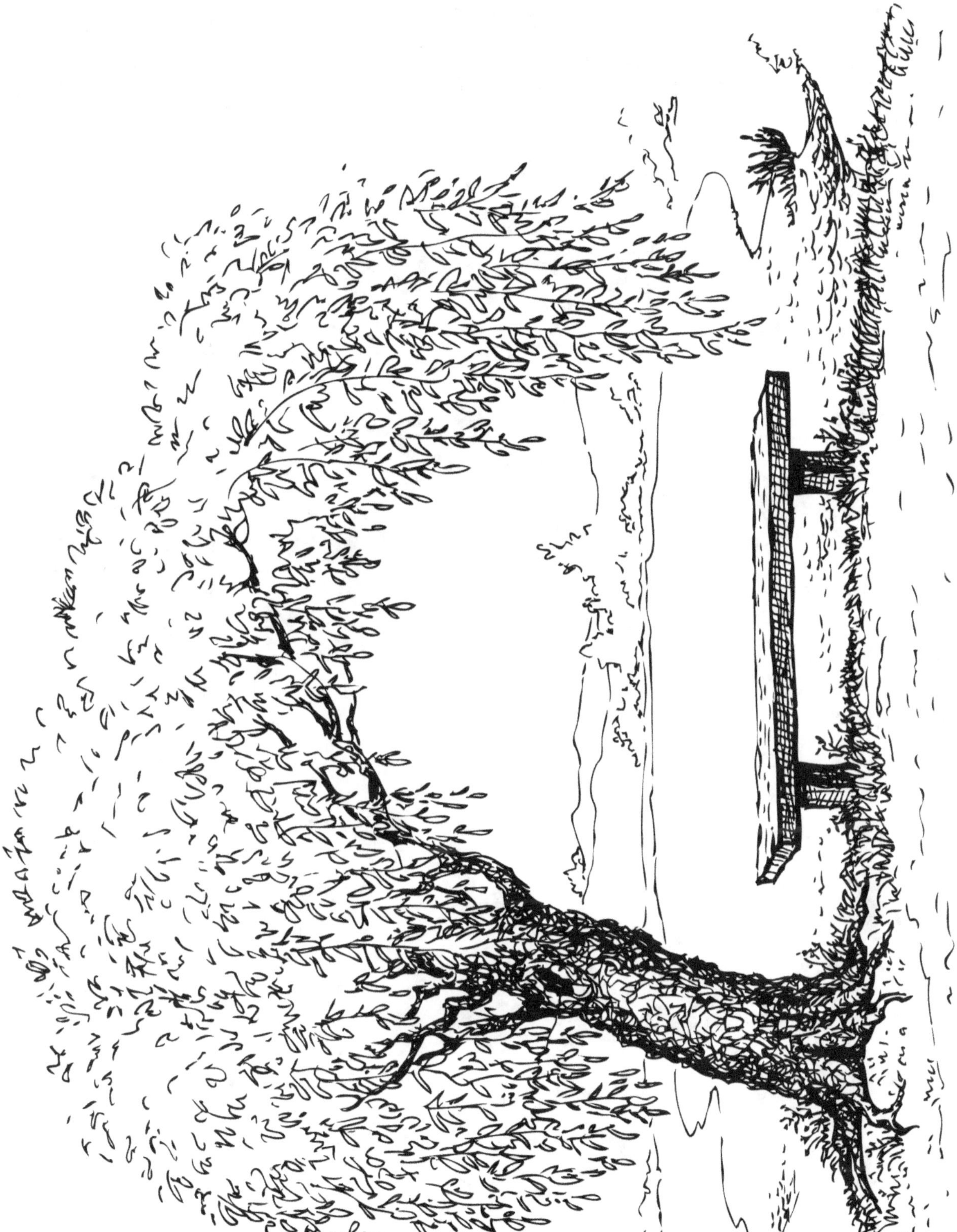

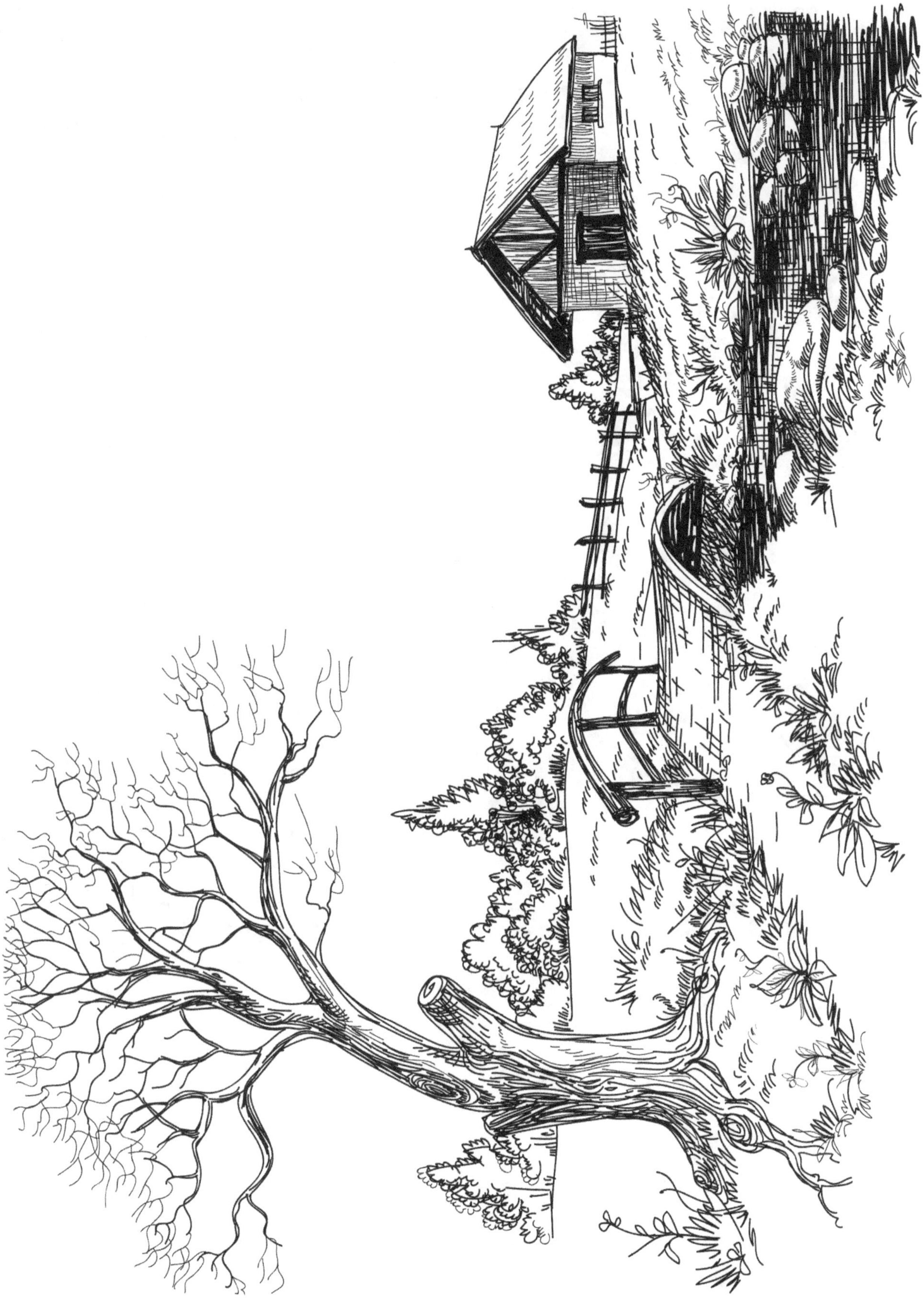

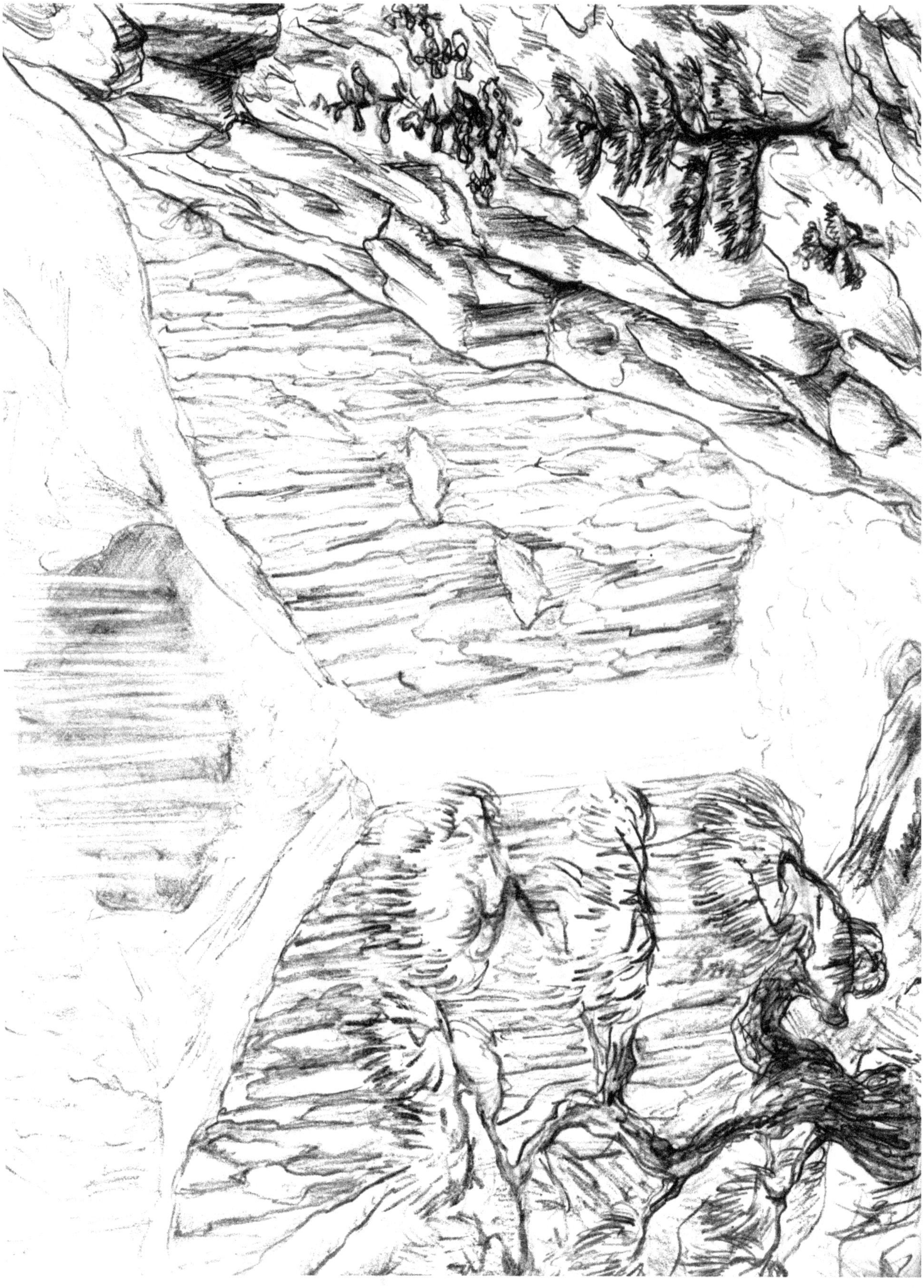

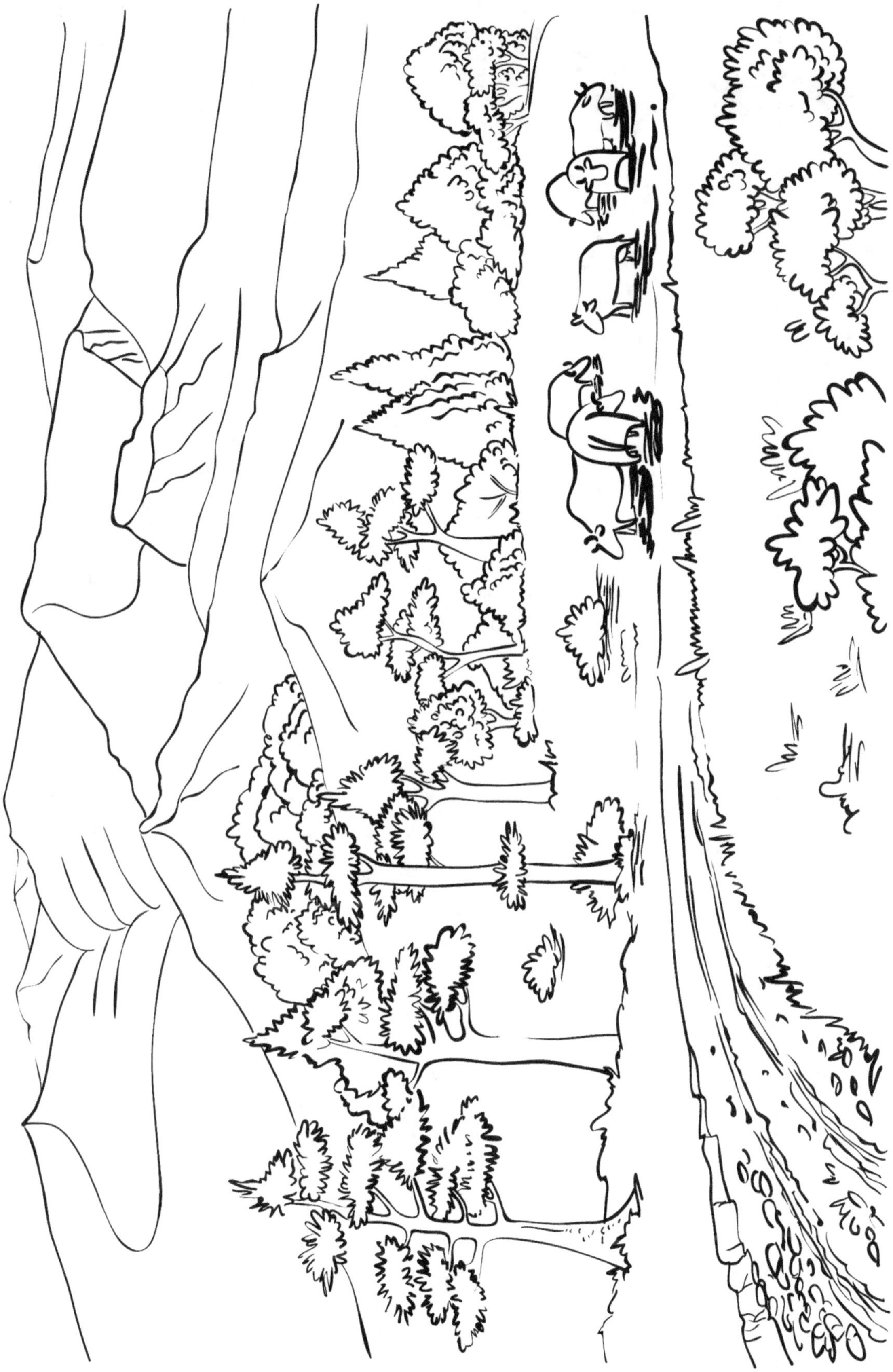

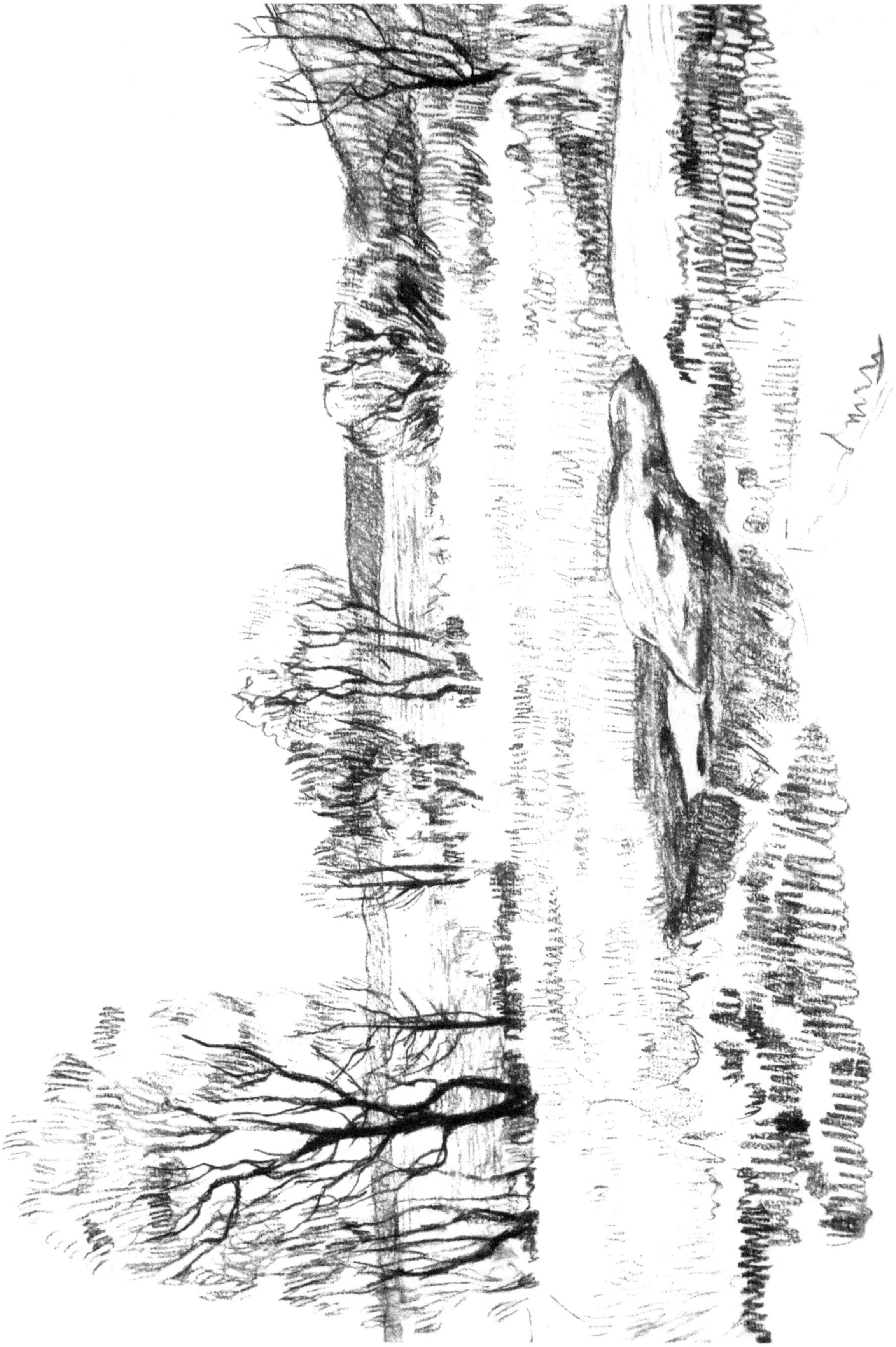

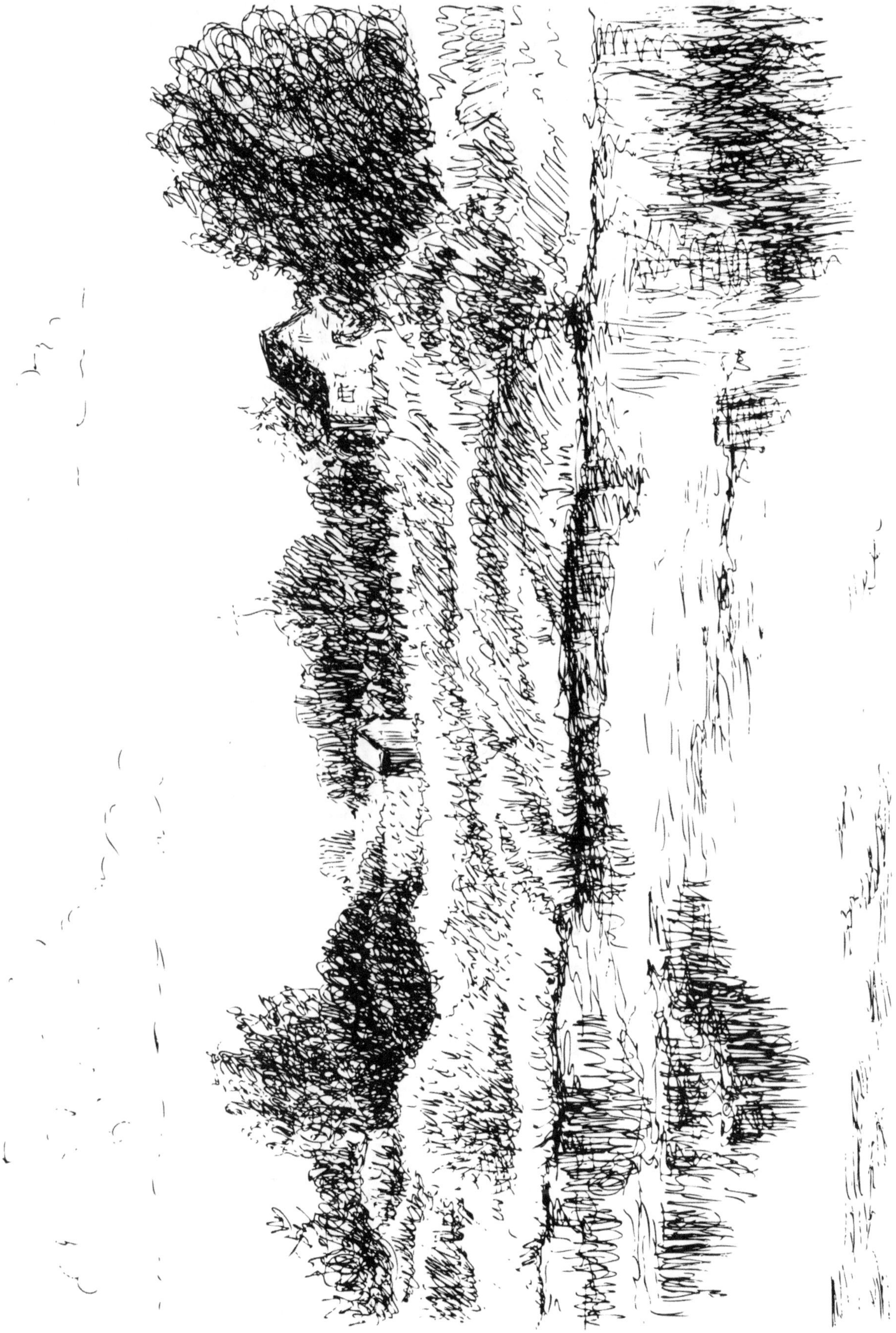

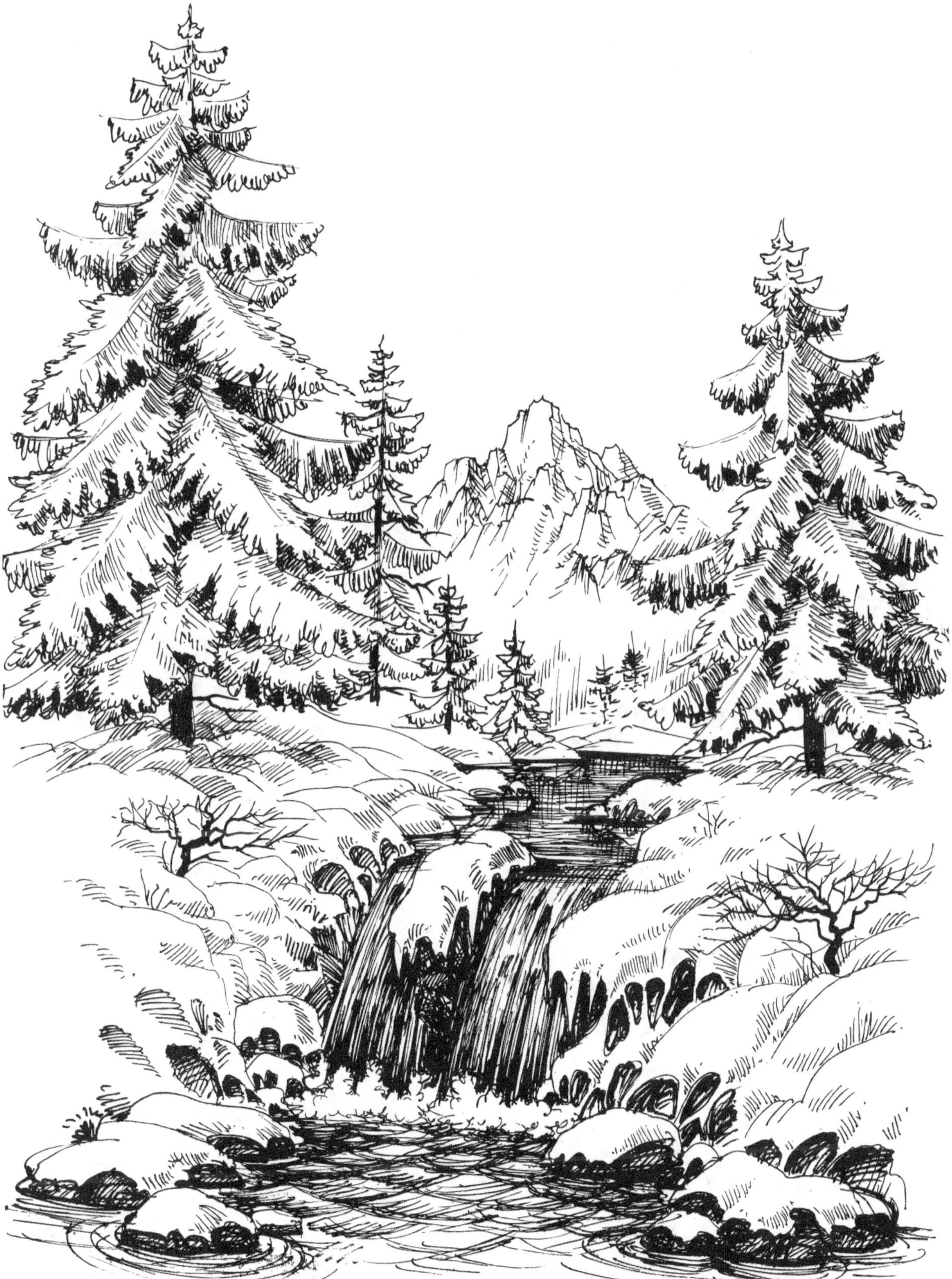

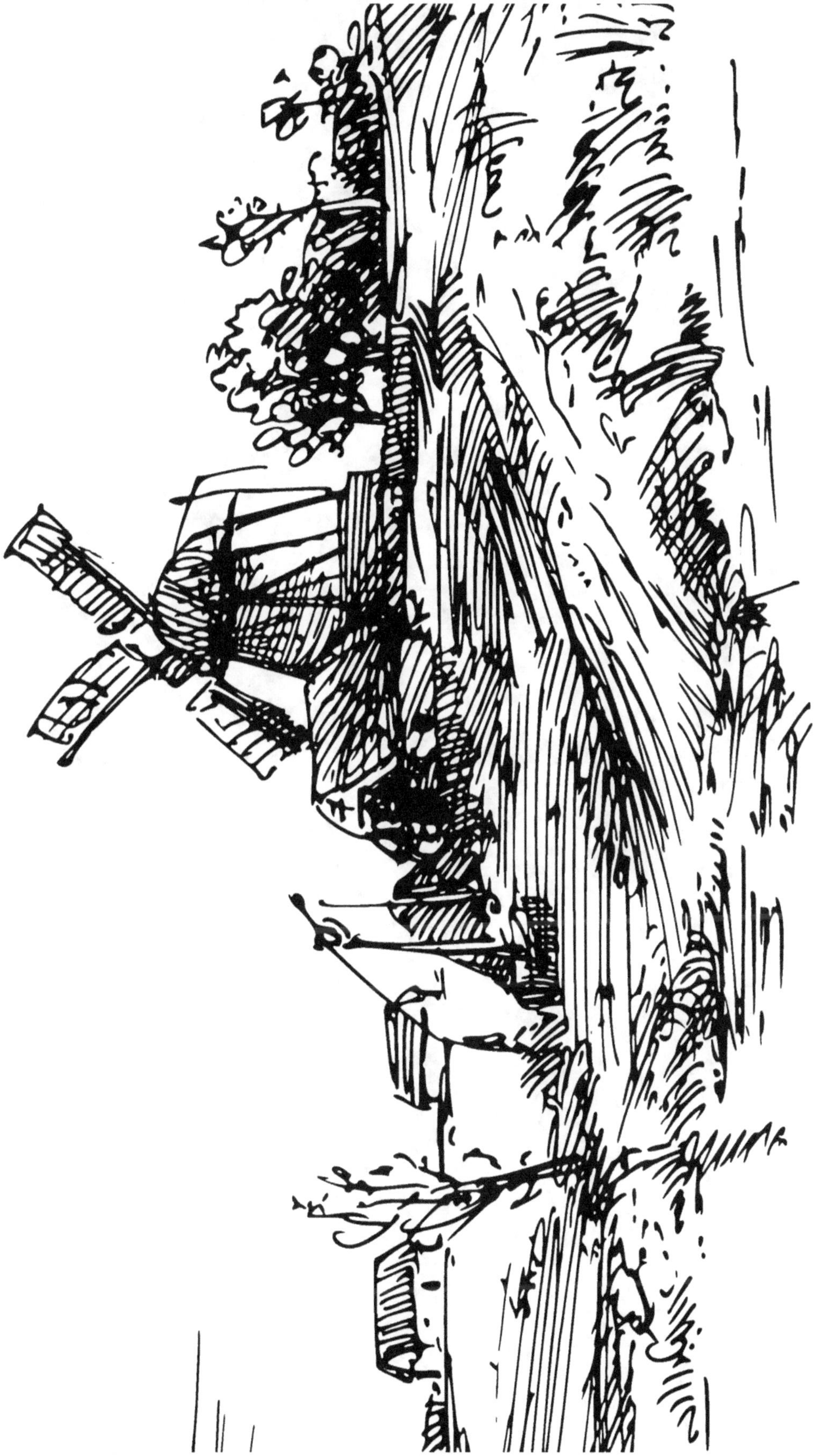

www.ingramcontent.com/pod-product-compliance
Lightning Source LLC
Chambersburg PA
CBHW081558170526
45166CB00009B/2734
* 9 7 8 1 5 1 9 6 2 2 8 3 9 *